15

Discover Deptford

Discover
DEPTFORD
and
LEWISHAM

A comprehensive guide to DEPTFORD, NEW CROSS, BROCKLEY, LEWISHAM & LADYWELL

by DARRELL SPURGEON

GREENWICH GUIDE-BOOKS

Copyright © Darrell Spurgeon 1997

All rights reserved. No part of this book may be copied or otherwise reproduced, stored in a retrieval system, or transmitted, in any form or by any means, electronic, mechanical, photocopying, recording or otherwise, without the prior permission of the author.

First published in Great Britain 1997 by
Greenwich Guide-Books,
72 Kidbrooke Grove, Blackheath, London SE3 0LG
(phone 0181-858 5831)

Other volumes in the same series by the same author:
Volume I (first edition), covering Woolwich, Plumstead, Shooters Hill, East Wickham, Abbey Wood & Thamesmead (published 1990, out of print)
Volume II, covering Greenwich, Westcombe & Charlton (published 1991)
Volume III, covering Eltham, New Eltham, Mottingham, Grove Park, Kidbrooke & Shooters Hill (published 1992)
Volume IV, covering Bexley, Bexleyheath, Welling, Sidcup, Footscray & North Cray (published 1993)
Volume V, covering Crayford, Slade Green, Erith, Belvedere, Abbey Wood & Thamesmead (published 1995)
Volume VI (new edition of Volume I), covering Woolwich, The Royal Arsenal, Woolwich Common, Plumstead, Shooters Hill & Abbey Wood (published 1996)
In preparation: Sydenham, Forest Hill, Catford, Hither Green

Front cover photograph is St Pauls Church (Thomas Archer, 1713-23)
gazetteer reference Deptford 3

Printed in Great Britain by Short Run Press, Exeter

A catalogue record for this book is available from the British Library
ISBN 0 9515624 6 0

CONTENTS

Foreword   page 7

DEPTFORD
Introduction   11
Section 'A' (High Street, Broadway & Creekside)   15
Section 'B' (Deptford Strand)   25
Section 'C' (New Town & St Johns)   35
Suggested Walks   40

NEW CROSS
Section 'A' (New Cross Gate)   43
Section 'B' (Canals & Railways)   48
Section 'C' (New Cross)   51
Section 'D' (Telegraph Hill)   56
Suggested Walks   58

BROCKLEY
Introduction   60
Section 'A' (Upper Brockley)   63
Section 'B' (Brockley Cross to Crofton Park)   67

LEWISHAM
Introduction   69
Section 'A' (Lewisham North & Loampit Hill)   73
Section 'B' (Ladywell & Lewisham South)   81
Suggested Walks   88

Notes on some Architects & Artists   90
Bibliography   92
Index   93

MAPS
Deptford & Lewisham   6
Deptford general map   10
Deptford Section 'A'   16
Deptford Section 'B'   26
Deptford Section 'C'   34
New Cross general map   44
Brockley general map   62
Lewisham general map   70
Lewisham Section 'A'   74
Lewisham Section 'B'   82

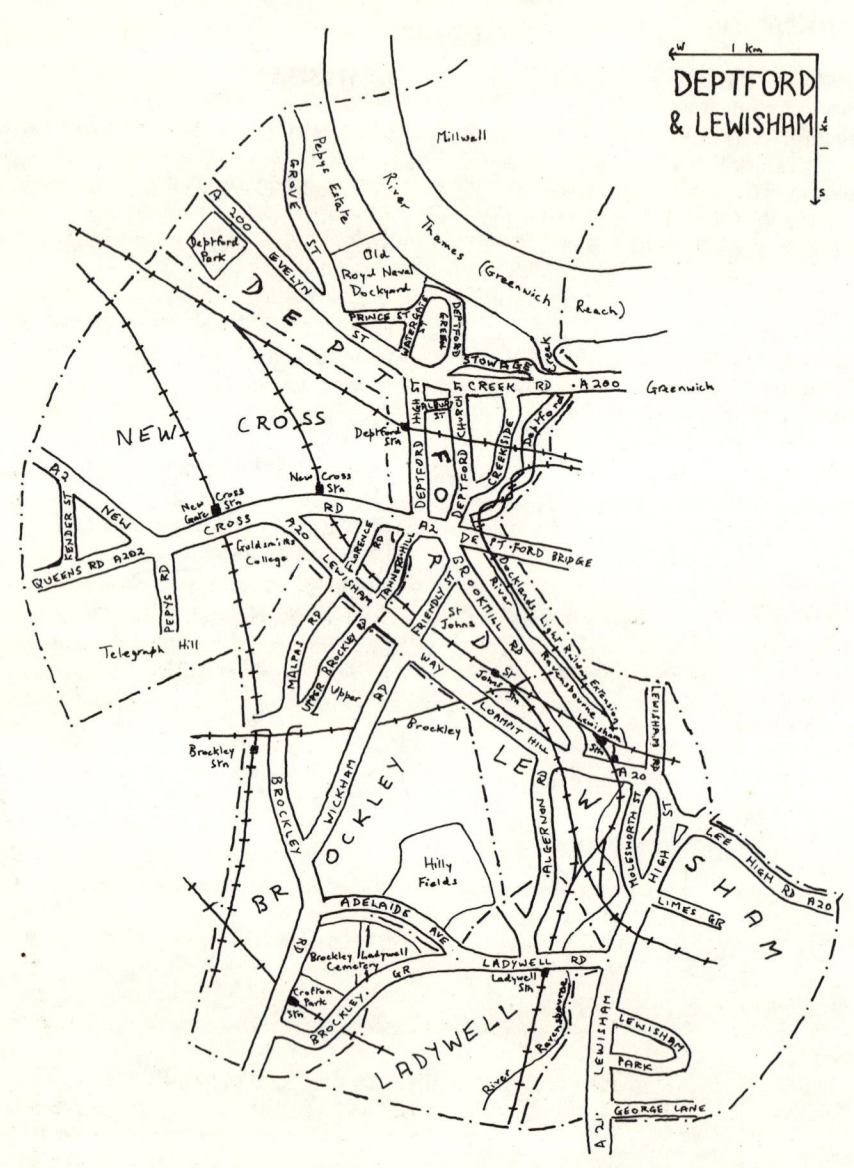

FOREWORD

This book covers five areas - Deptford, New Cross, Brockley, Lewisham and Ladywell. The boundaries between the areas, which are topographical and not administrative boundaries, are shown on the map opposite.

The areas are predominantly in the London Borough of Lewisham; the only exception is the area north of Albury Street and Creek Road between Deptford Creek and Watergate Street, which is in the London Borough of Greenwich.

The London Borough of Lewisham was created in 1965 by the merger of the Metropolitan Boroughs of Deptford and Lewisham, which had been set up in 1900. The New Cross area was transferred to Deptford from the Metropolitan Borough of Camberwell in 1902. Before 1889, when the London County Council was formed, the boundary between Kent and Surrey ran across the New Cross area, in fact cutting through the grounds of Goldsmiths College.

The whole area is in a state of transition. Lewisham 2000, a scheme which involved improvement of the Town Centre and major traffic diversion, has recently been completed *(see page 72)*. Deptford City Challenge, a regeneration project, is now nearing completion *(see page 14)*. Creekside Renewal, another regeneration project, has just commenced *(see pages 22-23)*; it covers both the Deptford and Greenwich sides of Deptford Creek, and embraces the massive Greenwich Reach development on both sides at the mouth of the Creek. Work has recently commenced on the extension of the Docklands Light Railway from the Isle of Dogs to Deptford and Lewisham; its route is indicated on the map opposite, and on the map on page 34.

The basic framework for the areas of Deptford, New Cross, Brockley and Lewisham consists of a brief introduction, gazetteer, map(s), and (except in the case of Brockley) suggested walk(s). Ladywell, though a distinct area, is very close to the centre of Lewisham, and so is treated as part of Lewisham. Each location in the gazetteers is identified (using location numbers) on a map. There are suggested walks where places of interest are concentrated within an area which makes walking practicable and interesting.

Deptford is divided into three sections - Section 'A' High Street, Broadway & Creekside; Section 'B' Deptford Strand; and Section 'C' New Town & St Johns. There is a general map, showing the boundaries between each section, as well as a separate map for each section. There are suggested walks which cover most locations in each section.

New Cross is divided into four sections - Section 'A' New Cross Gate; Section 'B' Canals & Railways; Section 'C' New Cross; and Section 'D' Telegraph Hill. One map covers all sections, and the suggested walks cover most locations in Sections 'A' and 'C'. There is no separate introduction to New Cross, as it is covered by the Introduction to Deptford.

Brockley is divided into two sections - Section 'A' Upper Brockley; and Section 'B' Brockley Cross to Crofton Park. One map covers both sections; there are no suggested walks.

Lewisham is divided into two sections - Section 'A' Lewisham North & Loampit Hill; and Section 'B' Ladywell & Lewisham South. Ladywell is thus included in Section 'B'. There is a general map, showing the boundaries between the two sections, as well as a separate map for each section. There are suggested walks which cover most locations in each section.

Although the introductions to the areas contain some historical background, and certain locations have some historical information in indented paragraphs, the guide is not a history of Deptford and Lewisham, and makes no pretensions to be a work of local history. Again, although some non-specialist knowledge of architecture is assumed, the guide does not become involved in detailed architectural analysis, and a conscious attempt has been made to avoid architectural jargon. Readers interested in further information on local history and architectural detail may like to consult the list of books at the end of the guide.

The gazetteers are intended as a comprehensive list of buildings and landscape features which are of visual interest, though the choice of places is inevitably very personal. The emphasis is on what is there now, not so much on what has been there in the past, and practical information is given on how best to see each place.

The maps, which are the key to the guide, adopt the same practical approach. Virtually every place mentioned in the text is pinpointed on a map in such a way as to make it easy to find and notice. The maps are indicative and not necessarily to scale, and only show those roads which are likely to be important to the visitor. It is suggested that a proper and more detailed road map of the area be obtained.

The starring system in the gazetteers enables visitors to allocate their time to the best advantage. All locations which are starred are, in my opinion, worth a very special effort to see. The stars are from one up to three, depending on my assessment of their interest and importance. Most locations however are not starred; this does not mean they are not worth seeing, such places invariably have interesting features and help to make the area distinct.

Italics are used for information on access, for other practical advice, for introductory notes before the walks, and also for cross-referencing. Paragraphs with information of a specifically historical nature are indented.

The sequence of locations in the gazetteers broadly follows the order in the suggested walks, and locations not included in the walks are slotted into the sequence in a way which would make it more convenient for a visit.

Some locations are difficult of access, and the guide gives practical information on how to overcome this difficulty. In some cases this may not always be possible, but it is certainly worth trying. In other cases, a certain initiative is demanded; for example, it is usually necessary to phone or call at the clergyman's residence to obtain access to church interiors. In my experience most clergymen are extremely helpful in facilitating this. And many places which are private will not in practice turn away the interested visitor asking permission to view. The text includes contact telephone numbers and/or addresses which may be found helpful in this context.

Of the publications which I have consulted, I wish to make particular mention of 'London 2: South', by Bridget Cherry and Nikolaus Pevsner, in the Penguin Buildings of England series; the Department of the Environment List of Buildings of Architectural & Historic Interest, which can be consulted at the National Monuments Record (London office), 55 Blandford Street, London W1; 'Turning the Tide, a history of everyday Deptford', by Jess Steele; 'Retracing Canals to Croydon & Camberwell', by Brian Salter; and 'Lewisham, History & Guide', by John Coulter. These and other publications which I have found useful are listed in the bibliography at the end.

I wish to give very special thanks and acknowledgment to numerous local people who helped me in various ways.

This book would not be so replete with factual information were it not for the help I have received from John Coulter, of the Local Studies Centre at Lewisham Library, Lewisham High Street. I have learned so much from his various publications on Lewisham (particularly the one mentioned above), he has answered what must have seemed to him an endless stream of questions, he has saved me from going astray on numerous occasions, and he has devoted his expertise to considerable research on my behalf. I cannot emphasise too strongly how much I owe to John.

Jean Wait, the Borough Archivist at the Local Studies Centre, also dealt courteously and efficiently with my many requests for information. Both Jean and John read the draft text in full; Jess Steele read the draft text on Deptford and New Cross, Gillian Heywood the text on Brockley, and John King (of the Lewisham Local History Society) the text on Lewisham. All offered many useful suggestions and much constructive criticism.

Many thanks also to Philip Ashford, of Lewisham Planning; Colin Mclean, of Deptford City Challenge; Patrick Codd, the Lewisham Town Centre Manager; Albert Tothill, Property Manager, Convoys Wharf; Jill Goddard, of Creekside Renewal; Ken White, for lots of interesting bits of information; Mr & Mrs Jonathan Horsfall-Turner; John West; Julian Watson; Len Reilly; Diana Rimel; Jim Packer; Jeff Galvan, Capital Planning Manager, Lewisham Hospital; Christine Speranza and Brian Nurse, of Thames Water.

Many thanks also to Jim Pope for invaluable advice on production and design; and to Roy Atterbury (of Anchor Displays, Eltham) for much good advice, and together with Luke Puplett, for expert processing of the photographs.

The area covered by this guide, like any urban area, is subject to the process of change, and the situation with regard to the condition and function (or even the existence) of buildings, their accessibility etc can change quite rapidly. However, the information was checked before going to print, and if anyone is misled in any way, I can only offer my apologies.

Darrell Spurgeon,

Blackheath, August 1997

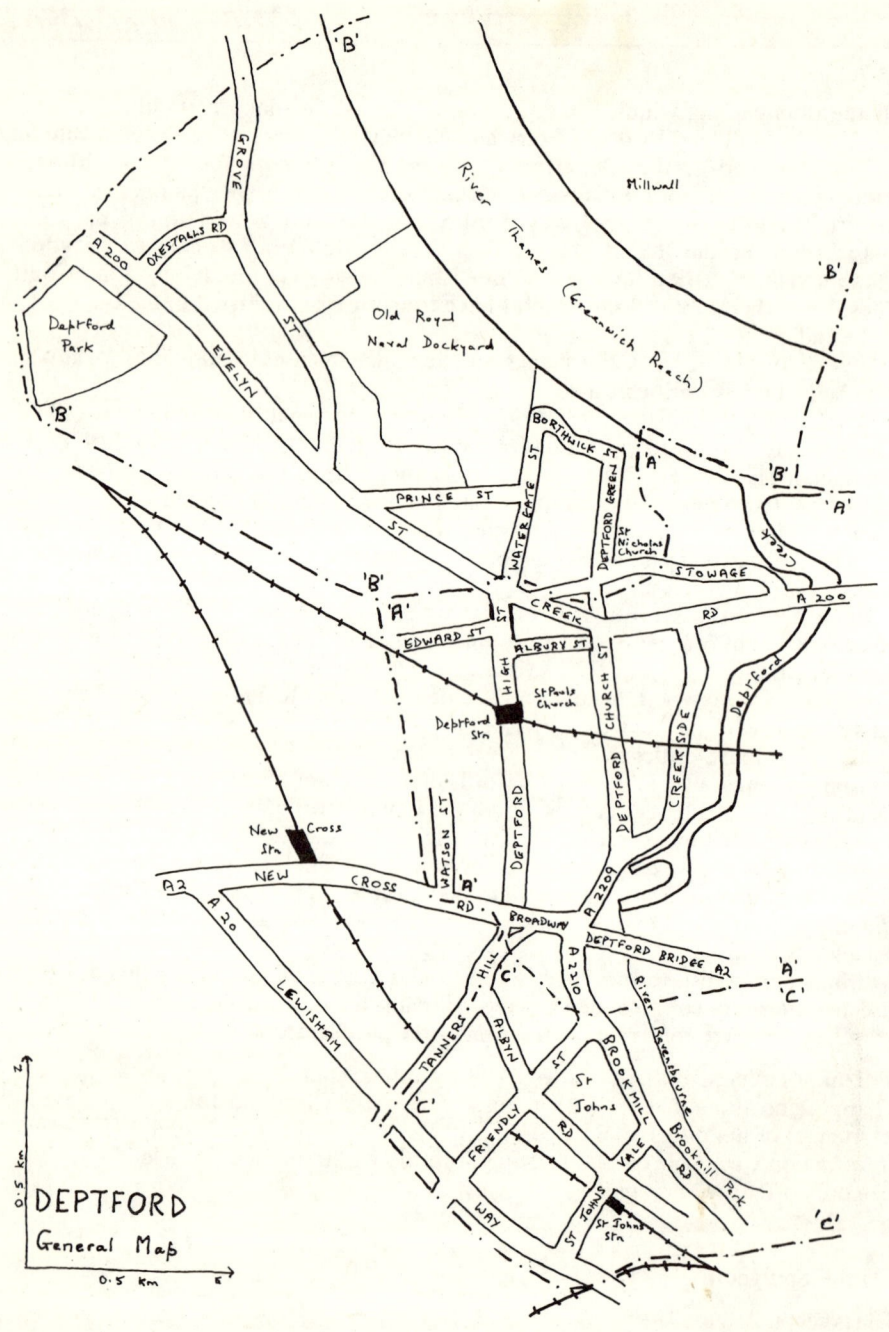

DEPTFORD

Introduction

In the Tudor period Deptford became a place of outstanding importance in British naval and maritime history, and it is only in this century that this historical link has been severed. From medieval times there had been two centres of settlement - Deptford Strand, along the riverside and Deptford Creek; and Deptford Town, around Deptford Bridge and the Broadway.

Throughout the Georgian period Deptford was an important town in its own right. It was quite separate from Greenwich to the east, for Deptford Creek was a very positive barrier; there was no direct road link between the historic centres of Deptford and Greenwich until Deptford Creek Bridge was constructed in 1815.

From the mid 19th century Deptford inevitably became entangled in the growth of London. However, it retains today a distinct identity, with many old buildings and historical sites, within a corner bounded by the Thames, the Creek and the route of Watling Street; and the two old centres remain focal points today.

Deptford Creek is the tidal and navigable part of the River Ravensbourne *(see Lewisham Introduction, page 69)*. The Creek starts just north of Deptford Bridge and flows under Deptford Creek Bridge before joining the Thames.

Roman to medieval times

Watling Street, the Roman road from Dover, forded the Creek where Deptford Bridge is now; it continued roughly along the line of the A2 to London. There have been Roman finds at several points around Broadway, the southern end of the High Street, and New Cross Road.

In 1992 a Saxon cemetery (the closest to the centre of London yet discovered) was excavated on the site of the Dover Castle pub, Deptford Broadway.

During the medieval period there was a village devoted to fishing and the building of small boats along the riverfront, known as Deptford Strand. St Nicholas Church was nearby at Deptford Green, and to the west was the manor house of Sayes Court. There were a number of corn-mills along Deptford Creek down to Deptford Bridge, where a wooden bridge had been erected at least by the mid 14th century, and around here was a small settlement.

The Dockyard and the Victualling Yard

In 1513 Henry VIII decided to set up the Royal Naval Dockyard on a site to the west of Deptford Strand. It expanded quickly, and became known as the Kings Yard; it was the principal dockyard in the country until the end of the century, when it began to be overtaken by Chatham.

Naval warehouses had been set up at an adjoining site further up-river about the same time as the dockyard. The site was called the Red House by the early 17th century, and in 1742 the site became the main Navy Victualling Depot, manufacturing as well as storing provisions; it was renamed Royal Victoria Victualling Yard after the Queen's visit in 1858.

The two sites, though distinct, were naturally closely associated. Many of the great voyages of discovery, by Drake, Frobisher, Raleigh, and later by Cook were launched from the area. The dockyard closed in 1869, and the site is now Convoys Wharf, used for the import of newsprint, probably the most intensively used commercial area on the Thames in Inner London. The victualling yard outlasted the dockyard by nearly 100 years, closing in 1961; the site is now part of the Pepys Estate. A number of older buildings have survived on both sites.

The Stowage site

The Stowage site, extending from the street called Stowage to the River and the Creek, was of great importance in Deptford's maritime and industrial history.

In 1514, Henry VIII gave a charter to Trinity House, a guild of mariners, which had been founded at the Stowage, just east of St Nicholas Church, in 1511. The Corporation of Trinity House came to assume responsibility for licensing Thames pilots, for charting the coast, and for lighthouses and navigational structures throughout England and Wales. It moved to the City of London in 1660.

The East India Company was awarded a charter in 1600, granting it exclusive trading rights to the East Indies; ships were built and fitted out at their depot on Deptford Creek, as well as at private shipyards nearby. The Company moved from Deptford in 1782.

In 1825 the General Steam Navigation Company, which may have been the world's first commercial steamship company, was founded by the Creek. Several of their ships were built here and many others fitted out up to 1970.

In 1889 Deptford Power Station was built on the western part of the Stowage site by Sebastian de Ferranti. It was the world's first electric power station to generate at high tension beyond the local area; it transmitted power as far as the West End, as well as for tramways and electric trains. An extension in 1948 made it the second biggest power station in the country after Barking. It was finally demolished in 1992.

Upper Deptford

During the 18th century Deptford Broadway became an important shopping centre around the great triangular green which it then formed, and Deptford Church Street, which was also a major shopping street, expanded northwards to join up with the village of Deptford Strand. Deptford High Street (called Butt Lane until 1825) was a street of houses rather than shops until the mid 19th century.

The area came to be called Upper Deptford, and the new church of St Pauls was built by 1723 to cater for the increased population. (The older church of St Nicholas is the more interesting, but St Pauls is without doubt the more beautiful.)

The 18th century also saw the establishment of a number of industrial developments inland along the Creek and the River Ravensbourne. One still survives, the Waterworks in Brookmill Road; when it first opened in 1701, water was taken direct from the river, but after 1862 the water came from wells sunk into the chalk. A gin distillery was set up at Deptford Bridge in 1779, and did not close until 1971; the site is now an industrial estate, though an original building remains. Other industry along Creekside was largely concerned with chemicals and gas.

In 1836 the great viaduct of the Greenwich Railway, London's first suburban railway, reached Deptford; the station was constructed on a bridge over the High Street. The original buildings have not survived, but this is London's oldest working railway station. This heralded the railway era; it was followed quite quickly by new railways which changed the face of Deptford and more particularly of New Cross.

New Cross and Hatcham

New Cross is a large area to the west of the original town of Deptford. Residential development was already spreading from London along New Cross Road from the 1820s, but later in the century the area to its north came to consist of pockets of housing within a maze of industrial sites and intersecting railway lines, sometimes known as the New Cross Railway Tangle.

New Cross had been a hamlet in the old parish of Deptford from at least the early 18th century. It is said to have taken its name from an inn, the New Cross House, near the junction of New Cross Road and Lewisham Way, a location now commonly known by the name of another old inn, the Marquis of Granby. The first tollgate of the New Cross Turnpike Trust was set up at the top of the present Clifton Rise in 1718; a century later it was moved to the west to the junction of New Cross Road and Queens Road, in the hamlet of Hatcham, an area now known as New Cross Gate.

The manor of Hatcham, which was in the old parish of Deptford, was purchased by the Haberdashers Company in 1614. The area to the north of the hamlet, which included the old manor house of Hatcham Park, was not intensively developed until after the demolition of the house in 1869. The area to the south which led up to Telegraph Hill was developed between 1875 and 1900; it was to include the two Haberdashers Askes schools, now known as Hatcham College.

The growth of industry

Canals had in fact reached Deptford and New Cross before the railways. Construction of the Grand Surrey Canal began in 1802 at the Surrey Docks, and reached Camberwell in 1811, a much shorter distance than originally planned; it did not close until 1971. At New Cross it formed a junction with the Croydon Canal, built 1807-09; this canal was purchased in 1836 for the construction of the Croydon Railway.

In 1839 New Cross Railway Station, later to be called New Cross Gate, was opened on the Croydon Railway; the southern part of the line from London Bridge to the new station was built on the bed of the disused Croydon Canal. A great area of locomotive sheds and workshops developed alongside the new station. George England, the pioneer locomotive builder, opened his works at Pomeroy Street in 1840. A branch to Deptford Wharf was opened in 1849.

In 1850 another station called New Cross, further to the east, opened on the North Kent Line. From 1869 both stations were linked by the East London Railway through a Thames tunnel to Wapping. The South London Line, opened 1866 from London Bridge to Peckham, marks the western boundary of the area.

Industrial development received a boost with the coming of the railways. A multitude of 19th century firms in the New Cross area have closed and have left no trace; but at some sites older buildings from firms which have disappeared have survived - the Mazawattee Tea Company works, which opened in 1901; the Stones engineering works, which moved in 1881 from the railway arches at Deptford Station; Clark Bunnett, engineering works which started in the 1820s; and, on the Deptford riverside, the John Penn marine engineering works of c1860.

Deptford New Town

The name New Town was first given to an area broadly between Tanners Hill and Friendly Street. The northern part was developed 1805-1815, the first large development to the south of the Dover Road; this part was demolished after the war. The southern part was developed in the 1840s; Lucas Street, the adjoining terraces in Albyn Road, and some terraces in Friendly Street have survived.

New Town was developed further east, between Friendly Street and St Johns Vale, between 1855 and 1875, and this is the area which has best survived; many terraces and groups are of a high standard of design, and have been generally well preserved. This area is nowadays known as St Johns - St Johns Church with its tall spire was built in 1854, and St Johns Station opened in 1873.

Deptford today

Deptford is now nearing the end of a programme of regeneration, Deptford City Challenge, which started in 1992. Among specific environmental improvements have been the restoration of a number of older buildings in the Broadway and the High Street, new buildings in key locations in a sympathetic style, demolition of some tower blocks and the restoration of others on the Milton Court Estate, refurbishment of tower blocks on the Pepys Estate, a new site for Millwall Football Club and housing on the old site, as well as numerous community and training initiatives.

Another regeneration programme, Creekside Renewal, has just started in the area of Deptford Creek. Projects include a riverside walk and footbridges across the creek, a large housing estate at Stowage, and a major retail and leisure development, including a hotel and a cruise liner terminal, on the Greenwich side. The Docklands Light Railway extension to Lewisham, due for completion by 2000, will run through Creekside and Brookmill Park, with stations at Deptford Bridge and Elverson Road.

Deptford has no modern shopping centre to compete with Lewisham, Surrey Quays or Peckham. But Deptford High Street remains a lively shopping street, dominated by its market three days a week, and relatively unaltered by modern retailing patterns. New Cross Road (the A2), which runs for over two kilometres through the area, is an interesting mix of houses and shops, many of the houses being fine Georgian and early Victorian survivals, and many of the shops having modern shopfronts on older buildings. Lewisham Way, which links Deptford and Lewisham, continues the pattern of groups of fine 19th century houses, and has several separate buildings of great interest. Evelyn Street, the other main road through the area, has less appeal, being dominated by postwar housing estates.

Deptford has a number of further and higher education colleges, many involved exclusively with or having a strong emphasis on the arts - Goldsmiths College, the Laban Centre, Lewisham College and its new Deptford campus, the Rachel McMillan Building of the University of Greenwich, Rose Bruford College, Lewisham Academy of Music. There are also several art galleries, artists' studios and workshops.

DEPTFORD

Gazetteer

Section 'A' HIGH STREET, BROADWAY & CREEKSIDE
(See map on page 16)

1. *Deptford Station. This is London's oldest working railway station, but nothing remains of the original building. However, the ramp leading up to the station, the railway viaduct and part of the walkway alongside have survived.

> The London and Greenwich Railway opened between Deptford Station and Spa Road Bermondsey in February 1836, a distance of four kilometres. It was London's first passenger railway; it was extended to London Bridge in December 1836, and to Greenwich in 1838. Spa Road Station closed in 1915.
>
> The railway runs on a long viaduct of brick arches (878 from London Bridge to Greenwich), designed by the engineer George Landmann. The section from Deptford Station westwards to North Kent East Junction, Rolt Street *(see New Cross 16)*, is the original structure of 1836, and from Deptford Station eastwards to Norman Road Greenwich the original structure of 1838.
>
> Long sections of the route were flanked by a public walkway, in part lined by trees.

The present building on the High Street is largely of 1927, as are the platform canopies. The bridge across the High Street is of 1963.

In the yard to the south, on the west side of the High Street, can be seen the ***ramp (1A)**, or inclined plane, designed by George Landmann 1836; it was used for hauling up rolling stock to an engine shed after repair in the yard. The ramp runs parallel with the street, then turns sharply eastwards towards it; many of the arches are now occupied by small businesses. Besides the view from the yard, there is also a good view of the ramp in Douglas Way and along an adjacent footpath.

Opposite, and alongside **The Mechanics Arms**, an Edwardian pub with an octagonal cupola, is ***Mechanics Path (1B)**, the only substantial surviving section of the walkway which flanked the original railway viaduct. It extends alongside the viaduct to Deptford Church Street, with small businesses in many of the arches; the viaduct and walkway then continues through the Crossfield Estate *(see 12B)*.

2. *Deptford High Street has great atmosphere and character, and is a remarkable survival. It is one of few examples left in London of a High Street, which while remaining a shopping street has been hardly altered by modern retailing patterns.

The shopfronts are of course modern, though several have in recent years been well and sympathetically altered; but many buildings have older upper floors - often early or mid 19th century, and in a few cases late 17th or 18th century. The street is crossed by a bridge of the Greenwich Railway; the platforms on the bridge are of Deptford Station, London's oldest working railway station *(see 1)*. To the north of the

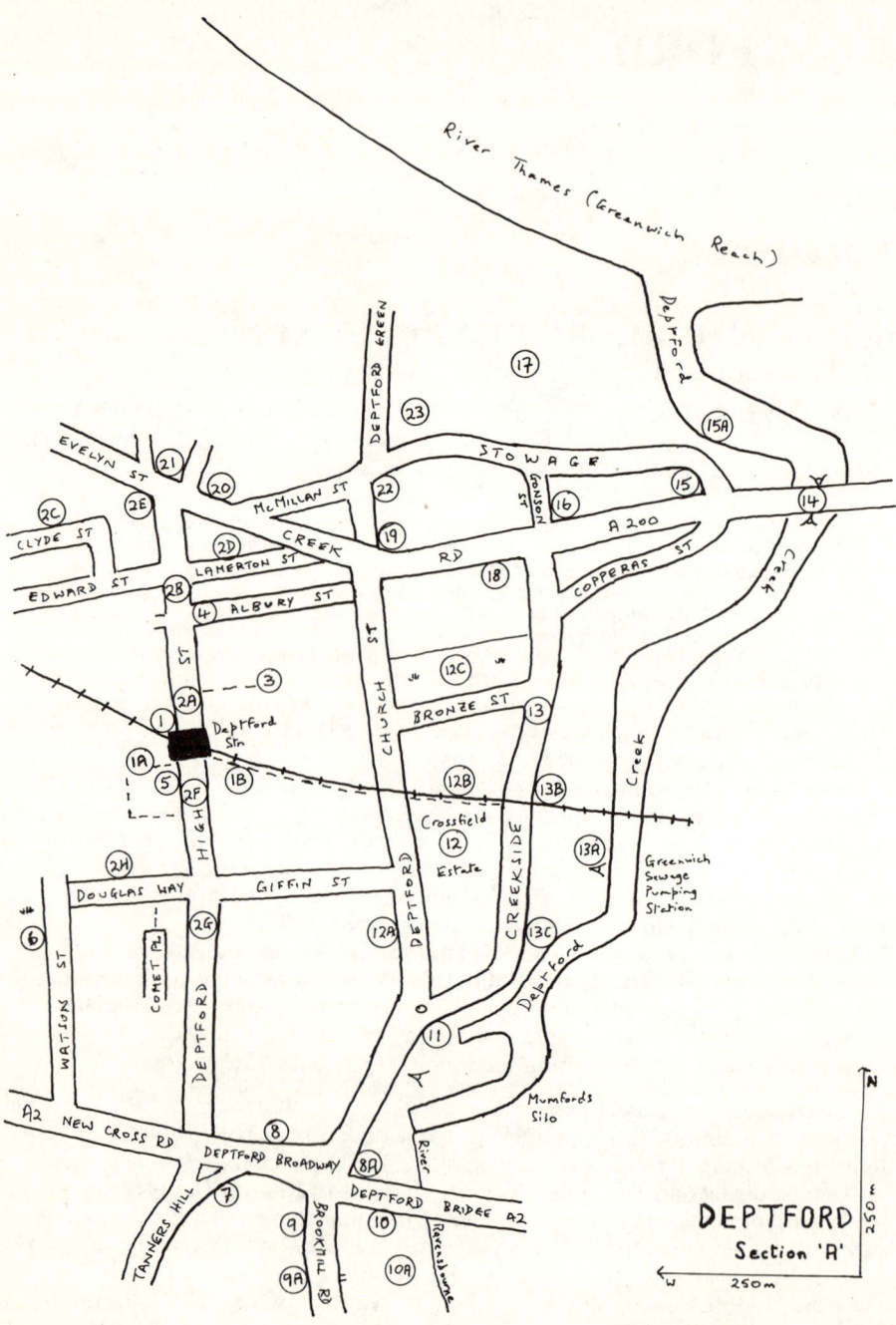

railway are St Pauls Church and Albury Street, both early 18th century. To the south the street is largely pedestrianised, the scene on Wednesdays, Fridays and Saturdays of the hectic **Deptford Market**, which spreads into Douglas Way (mainly second-hand goods) and Giffin Street. In this section is Our Lady of the Assumption Church. At the junction with Deptford Broadway is an old anchor, placed there 1988.

> Because of the abundance of buildings and features of interest, the entries for the High Street are split into blocks - two blocks going northwards from Deptford Station, with diversions into Clyde Street and Lamerton Street; then, two blocks going southwards from Deptford Station, with diversions into Douglas Way and Giffin Street. The even numbers are on the east side, the odd numbers on the west side.

Deptford Station north to Albury Street (2A):

Nos 147/153, a late 19th century group, with continuous windows along the first floor, which may indicate earlier use as a workshop.

No 144a has a plaque inscribed: 'Deptford Friends Meeting House stood here, demolished 1907, Peter the Great Tsar of Russia worshipped here 1697-8.' (He was actually in Deptford for several months in early 1698, *see 28*.) The present building, faced with white and green stone tiles, is of 1926.

Nos 150/152 are probably late 18th century.

Nos 160/162, of 1846. A 17th century pub, Royal Oak, was formerly on the site. *For St Pauls Church, see 3.*

Nos 164/168, an imaginative development of flats and workshops of 1988.

Nos 167/169, a mid 18th century house, with a steep roof and dormers. No 167 has a modern shopfront, but no 169 has a bowed early 19th century shopfront which may be difficult to see because the shutters are often down. **Nos 163/165** are similar but not so old.

Nos 177/179, a handsome classical pair, probably c1840.

The Pilot, no 174, now called The Ballylane Inn, a tall and narrow classical pub, c1850.

Hamilton Place, nos 181/195, a unified composition of 1844, with well-preserved upper floors.

For Albury Street, see 4.

Albury Street north to Evelyn Street / Creek Road (2B)

No 197, a mid 19th century building, was formerly the booking hall of **Deptford Electric Palace Cinema,** which was open from 1910 to 1954; the cinema building is still there at the back, and is now a night-club.

Nos 201/203 is basically a late 17th century timber-framed house, the front having been altered later, now in poor condition.

Off Edward Street, there are in **Clyde Street (2C)** two distinctive interwar buildings: **Old Town Library**, now Old Town Community, Arts & Youth Centre, a building of 1931 with classical features; and the adjoining red brick **Deptford Public Baths**, of 1925, which closed in 1988. The future of both buildings is uncertain.

Lamerton Street (2D), a narrow cobbled street, has on both sides a sequence of strange houses of 1989 with colourful post-modernist porches.

The White Swan, no 217, now called Maimie O'Learys. There has been a pub on the site since the 18th century; it formerly incorporated a music-hall. The present attractive building is basically early 19th century, though the roofline and ground floor were altered later. Note the swan at the corner apex.

No 223, a fine building c1828, formerly a pub called the Red Cow. The buildings on either side are also basically early 19th century.

The Noahs Ark (2E), 412 Evelyn Street, a handsome pub, probably of the early 1840s, nicely rounding the corner.

Deptford Station south to Douglas Way / Giffin Street (2F):
For Our Lady of the Assumption Church, see 5.
Nos **127/129**, a handsome and well-preserved pair, c1800.

St Pauls House, no 125, now a social services office. An intriguing brick building, with all sorts of odd features; it was built 1914 as the Rectory for St Pauls, and remained in this use until 1949.

Nos 104/118 are basically a long 18th century unified composition above modern shopfronts, apart from the intrusion of the totally modern nos 110/114.

Nos 111/119 are an attractive Italianate mid 19th century group. **Nos 107/9** on the opposite side of Douglas Way are part of the same development.

Douglas Way / Giffin Street south to Deptford Broadway (2G):
Douglas Way and Giffin Street have wide empty open spaces which, whilst in use on market days, otherwise do not fit in with the character of the High Street.

Giffin Street has elaborate street furniture; it leads to **Wavelengths**, a low, bright but uninspired building of 1991, combining a swimming pool and a library.

Douglas Way leads to **The Albany Centre and Theatre (2H)**, a low-lying building of 1982.

> The present building acts as a community centre, a theatre and a base for community arts projects. The Albany Institute was set up by the Deptford Fund charity in 1894; it provided a comprehensive system of welfare for young women and children of Deptford, extending to men and incorporating adult education from the 1920s.

Note also in Douglas Way a long mural 'Deptford Railway Yard and High Street c1840', by South London Murals 1981. To the south, an old cobbled footpath leads to an old granary in **Comet Place**, probably basically late 18th century, but derelict.

Nos 32/44, a low 18th century group with dormers in the roofs, much altered.

No 13, of 1838, is very imposing; it has a great bow through two upper floors, and a porch with two pairs of Ionic columns, but is spoilt by an appalling modern shopfront.

3. ***St Pauls Church. One of the most powerful baroque churches in Britain - 'large, sombre and virile' (Pevsner), the masterpiece of Thomas Archer, set in a large churchyard which gives fine views of the church from all sides.

> One of the few of the Queen Anne churches of 1711 actually built; it was designed by Thomas Archer. Work began 1713, and it was finally completed 1723. There have been several restorations, but it has been hardly altered, externally or internally.

The church is encased in dazzling white Portland stone. On approaching from the High Street, the view is dominated by the great semi-circular portico of giant Tuscan columns, approached by five staircases. The portico is surmounted by a balustrade from which the steeple rises in stages (note the urns), from a graceful round tower to a slender spire, with a copper vase and gilt weather vane at the top.

The sides of the church are each like grand entrance fronts in their own right, with Palladian double staircases leading to the entrance doors (now closed) and pediments above giant rusticated pilasters; these pilasters are continued round the walls. The rear has a semi-circular apse with a curved Venetian window and pediment.

The ***interior** is outstanding too, and very theatrical. *The church is normally open Wednesday, Friday and Saturday afternoons, 1400 to 1600, otherwise contact 0181-692 1419, or 692 0989.* The entrance is through the portico and under the tower; after emerging from the narrow rounded vestibule under the tower, the immediate impression is of spaciousness, symmetry and dignity with light pouring in through the tall clear windows. The nave is virtually square; it is flanked on each side by two giant free-standing stone Corinthian columns separating the nave from the aisles, with panelled oak galleries above (smaller than Archer's original design). There are 12 additional columns - two engaged at an oblique angle under each corner, one on either side of the entrance, and one on either side of the apse - making 16 giant Corinthian columns in all.

At each corner is a circular chamber, fronted by a private box, and the oblique angle of the columns against these, together with the shallow apse, gives an almost oval effect to the interior. The two west chambers enclose spiral staircases leading to the galleries and the private boxes. The north gallery provides a fantastic view over the interior; the south gallery normally remains closed. The Corinthian pilasters along the aisles echo the giant columns. There are smaller wooden Corinthian columns under each of the four private boxes, and under the organ at the west end. The apse has a curved Venetian window. The windows are tall and round-headed, except for circular windows above the side entrances.

The furnishings and monuments are, in such a grand setting, relatively insignificant. However, there are some interesting monuments in the chancel alongside the apse: on the north side - Maria Finch 1745 with coloured marble rococo decoration, and Admiral John Sayer 1776 by Joseph Nollekens; on the south side - Elizabeth Bell 1809, Matthew Ffinch 1745, and above (though difficult to see) Dr Charles Burney, the literary scholar and collector, 1817 in a medallion against an obelisk. There is also a bust of Burney in the north-east circular chamber. A modern tablet on the south wall commemorates 'John Harrison, founder and first surgeon of the London Hospital who died in 1753 and was buried in this churchyard'. There is little stained glass: in the Venetian window, c1910; in a window over the north-west circular chamber, an 1813 figure of St Paul; and in each gallery, in the circular windows over the old doors, colourful windows by Alan Younger 1996 in memory of Father David Diamond, who had been Rector of Deptford 1969-92, and had involved the church deeply in community life and activity in the area.

Note also the fine intricate plasterwork on the oak ceiling, the mural by Henry Turner 1725 in the apse above the Venetian window, the coat of arms of Queen Anne on the organ, the elegant and impressive pulpit (designed by John James 1721, much cut down in size in 1873), and two box-pews; all these are of the original church. The Victorian romanesque font (of the 1840s, brought from Rochester Cathedral 1897) is the only major jarring addition. The reredos at the end of the north aisle is of 1916. The Stations of the Cross in white stone were brought here from St Michaels Ham Common in the early 1970s. The organ is of 1748, much altered in the 1930s. In the south aisle is a cannon from the Dockyard with the legend - 'Princess Margaret discharged this cannon to mark the opening of Deptford Festival 1971'.

The *****crypt** is contemporary with and extends the whole width of the church; the striking brickwork of the pillars and vaulted roof is by Thomas Lucas. It is normally open at lunchtime weekdays; entrances from the exterior are on both south and north sides, and from the interior in the south aisle.

The **churchyard** contains many table tombs and several gravestones. Just inside the west entrance, on the left, is a large tomb, probably 13th century, which was found during excavations in Brookmill Road 1868. At the east end is an obelisk to the Stone family 1807. Note also just to the north-west of the church the grave of Father David Diamond 1992, the only burial permitted in the churchyard since the 1850s.

The walls to the north and at the south-east corner are in part early 18th century. The walling beyond the south-east wall of the churchyard is of a former Baptist graveyard, and is also 18th century.

4. **Albury Street. This narrow, cobbled street is a distinctly metropolitan terraced street, a remarkable phenomenon in this area; it was laid out 1706-17 by the local bricklayer Thomas Lucas in what was then still a town outside London.

Most houses on the north side have survived relatively unaltered, apart from the loss of some decorative features; however, the frontages of nos 21, 33, 39 and 41 were rebuilt in the early 19th century, no 45 was rebuilt in the late 19th century, and nos 9/11 are recent infill, all in sympathetic style. On the south side only a small group has survived; the long gaps have been filled with pleasantly designed housing of the 1970s by the Greater London Council, at one point offering a wonderful view of St Pauls Church.

The older houses are of plum-coloured stock brick with red brick dressings; many have been well restored. They are mostly highly attractive, particularly the numerous houses which have retained a doorcase with panelled pilasters and a cornice hood on carved brackets; some brackets are very intricately and elaborately carved (in particular, nos 29 and 35 with angels heads, and also nos 37 and 43, nos 36 and 38).

Despite the gaps, rebuilds, and the loss of brackets and other decorative features, Albury Street remains of outstanding interest.

5. Our Lady of the Assumption Church. The nave of this Roman Catholic church was built in 1845; the chancel, chapel and sacristy were added in 1859. The frontage to the High Street has Gothic doors and very elongated Gothic windows, and piers reaching up to form pinnacles. At the rear, a wheel window faces west.

The ***interior** is attractive and has many delightful features. *The church is often open 1030 to 1130 on Saturday mornings, but it is best to telephone 0181-692 2011 beforehand to make an arrangement.* The orientation is to the west. The large crucifix in the porch is of c1871. The stone altar is of 1846, the richly decorated reredos of c1878, and the stained glass in the wheel window above of 1880. The mural of the Crucifixion above the chancel arch is of 1882. Another fine reredos in the Sacred Heart Chapel to the north of the chancel is of 1886. A pretty ogee-shaped doorway with a fine stone carving of the 'Descent into Hell', probably c1878, leads to the sacristy to the south of the chancel.

Two buildings which adjoin the church form a small square in front of the entrance - the **Presbytery**, no 131, of 1855, Italianate with a castellated parapet, and the **former porch**, c1860, with a Tudor-style archway, in use as the porch until c1980, since when it has been used only for storage.

6. Lewisham Academy of Music, Watson Street, occupies the former Coroners Court and Mortuary, two buildings of 1906 with strange decorative features. The two buildings will be linked as part of a redevelopment and expansion scheme currently under way.

The Academy is now in an isolated location with **Margaret McMillan Park**, a linear park stretching westwards, all around. Behind in the park is **Bridge and Banks**, a landscape sculpture with a stone bridge, by John Maine 1991.

7. *19/31 Tanners Hill. This low group is basically c1690. Many frontages have been rebuilt and most roofs have been restored, but the original appearance is largely preserved. **Nos 13/17** fit in with the group, but were built later.

8. *Deptford Broadway. This great triangular space at the western end of Deptford Bridge has an engaging mixture of older and modern buildings (if one disregards the old Skillcentre). As it is a major traffic junction, it is often difficult to appreciate that this is townscape of great character.

The numbering goes clockwise from the southern end of Deptford High Street.

The Centurion, no 1. This pub dates back at least to the mid 18th century. The present building is probably of 1889, and retains etched glass and some old fittings.

Nos 2/6 and **no 8** were developed by City Challenge c1993 in a sympathetic style. In the gap was Dover Castle, no 7, a pub of 1880 destroyed by an explosion in 1990; there had been a pub on the site since at least the 15th century.

Nos 9/14, now Antique Warehouse, form an interesting group. Nos 9/13 preserves the 1930s facade of a Burtons shop. No 14 is late 19th century, with elegant decorative features, and once formed part of Peppercorns Stores, which dominated the northern side of the Broadway at the turn of the century. The frontage of nos 15/16 adjoining dates from between the wars.

Nos 17/21 are a group of probably late 17th century origin, the present frontages being mid 19th century.

Nos 22/25, together with 1/11 Deptford Church Street, were developed by City Challenge c1995, in a style in sympathy with nos 17/21.

Deptford Campus (8A) of Lewisham College, formerly Deptford Skillcentre. This architectural disaster was built c1980 in vivid red brick, with a jagged centre and a peculiar overhanging upper floor on stone columns. The site behind, to the north, is where Deptford Creek begins *(see Introduction, page 11)*. The site will during 1998 be bisected by construction of the Docklands Light Railway extension.

The Fountain, no 36, a pub dating back at least to 1700; the present building is late 19th century, and is now called Noodle King.

Nos 41/2, National Westminster Bank, a handsome building, probably c1880.

No 47, basically late 17th century, altered in the 18th century, recently restored.

Nos 55/57, a handsome pair, probably c1840, recently restored.

9. Mereton Mansions, Brookmill Road. Formerly known as Carrington House, it was built by London County Council 1903 as a hostel for single men; it closed in 1991, and was in 1995 converted to flats. This is an impressive and monumental concave building, of red brick and white stone, following the curve in the road; the frontage is distinguished by the central canted oriel extending through five storeys up to a gable, two bowed oriels extending through four storeys, and end pavilions like towers with deep-eaved roofs.

The adjoining **Sylva Cottages (9A)** continue the curve in the road; they were also built in 1903 as part of the same project.

10. Deptford Bridge, over the River Ravensbourne, is now a structure of the 1970s. The road scene here will be transformed by the construction of a Docklands Light Railway station over the road by 1998.

> This is the site forded by the Romans for Watling Street. There was a wooden bridge here by 1345, it was rebuilt at least partly in stone 1570, and in iron 1883, and has been rebuilt many times since. Just to the north, in the grounds of the Deptford Campus, Deptford Creek ceases to be tidal and becomes the River Ravensbourne.

Dominating the area south of the bridge is **The Old Seager Distillery (10A)**, now a small industrial estate on the site of Seagers Gin Distillery.

> The Deptford Gin Distillery was opened as Goodhews Distillery in 1779, it became Hollands Distillery in the 19th century, and Seagers Distillery in 1919, when the whole premises were enlarged and modernised. It closed in 1971.

The entrance to the estate is now from Brookmill Road, through a site which was from the 1830s to 1905 **Norfolks Brewery**, no trace of which has survived.

The former entrance to the distillery was **14/16 Deptford Bridge**. This is an original distillery building of 1779, though the carriage entrance is late 19th century. This building is flanked by larger buildings which became part of Seagers - to the left an attractive block with some classical ornamentation, built as the furniture depot of Peppercorns Stores 1897 *(see 8)*, and to the right a neo-Georgian block, probably c1960. The old distillery buildings on the site behind are all either interwar or postwar; note International House, a well-designed building of the 1920s.

11. The Birds Nest, 32 Deptford Church Street, formerly the Oxford Arms, refronted in the late 19th century. It now incorporates a small theatre, the Birds Nest Theatre. In the early 19th century the Deptford Theatre adjoined the pub.

12. Crossfield Estate, an estate of large blocks built in the late 1930s, occupies a large area between Deptford Church Street and Creekside.

On the north side of Frankham House, the only large block to the west of Church Street, is **The Pink Palace (12A)**, a jolly mural featuring cherubs surrounded by modern artefacts in a classical setting.

Striding through the estate is a long section of George Landmann's original ***railway viaduct (12B)** of brick arches of 1838; this is the most attractive part of the whole structure, with most arches remaining open. The walkway through the estate alongside the viaduct is a continuation of Mechanics Path *(see 1B)*.

To the north of the estate is a wildlife site, **Sue Godfrey Nature Park (12C)**, partly on the site of Gibbs & Canning industrial pottery, demolished 1967; some pottery sherds have been set in concrete as part of a wall in the park.

13. Creekside and **Copperas Street** run alongside Deptford Creek, but there is at present no ready access to the Creek. There are views of the Creek on either side of Deptford Creek Bridge *(see 14)*, but they are at present rather unappealing.

However, this whole area will over the next few years be the scene of a largescale regeneration project, Creekside Renewal *(see also 17)*. Between Creekside / Copperas Street, on the Deptford side, and Norman Road, on the Greenwich side, proposals include cleaning up the Creek, repairing the Creek walls, several redevelopment projects, and replacing the Ha'penny Hatch, which was from 1836 to 1938 a foot bridge between Deptford and Greenwich alongside the railway over the Creek.

The area south of the railway line is at present in a state of upheaval because of the construction of the Docklands Light Railway extension, due for completion 2000.

The Greenwich Railway crosses the Creek on a lifting bridge, rebuilt 1963 but no longer in operation. This bridge can be viewed, if the yard gates are open, where the railway viaduct crosses the street Creekside; it can also be seen from a car park in the Faircharm Industrial Estate **(13A)**, which also provides a view across the Creek of the engine houses and coal sheds for Sir Joseph Bazalgette's Greenwich Sewage Pumping Station of 1862. A view of the Mumfords Flour Mills silo, designed by Sir Aston Webb 1897, also on the Greenwich side, can be obtained from the site behind the Deptford Campus *(see 8A)*.

Note also on the street Creekside, just north of the railway viaduct, **Love Over Gold (13B)**, a splendid long mural of 1989 by Gary Drostle, inspired by local pop group Dire Straits and the work of local schoolchildren.

To the south, at Harold Wharf **(13C)**, is an imposing industrial building c1900, formerly the Stewart & Dennis engineering factory, now converted to artists studios.

14. Deptford Creek Bridge, with its control tower alongside, was opened in 1954. The first footbridge was constructed here in 1804, and the first road bridge in 1815. The bridge is lifted several times weekly at high tide to allow boats to pass to Brewery Wharf, occupied by Prior Aggregates; the wharf can be seen clearly looking southwards from the bridge, it is immediately to the left on the Greenwich side.

15. The Hoy Inn, 193 Creek Road. A pub on this site has existed since at least 1777; the present building was refronted in the early part of this century. Behind the pub, on the street Stowage, is a passage leading to the **Hoy Inn Stairs (15A)** on Deptford Creek, owned by the pub. The stairs were used until the early 19th century for a ferry service across to the Greenwich side of the Creek.

Access to the stairs is blocked by an iron gate on Stowage. If you have a strong interest in viewing the stairs, ring Mr Hingston on 0181-692 3567 and it may be possible to arrange this.

16. The Duke, 125 Creek Road. An attractive pub, probably c1850.

17. Stowage. The street called Stowage still follows a winding route dating from the 17th century. The derelict site between the street and the river will (together with a similar derelict site on the Greenwich side of Deptford Creek) be transformed in the next few years by the **Greenwich Reach** development, linked with the regeneration programme called Creekside Renewal *(see also 13)*. The proposals include: cleaning up the creek, a riverside walk, and a community boatyard; a new Creekmouth footbridge to the Greenwich side, where a massive development designed by Broadway Malyan is proposed, including a cruise liner terminal, hotel, shopping, a cinema complex, and other leisure and entertainment facilities; and, on the Stowage site, a new housing development by Fairview Homes.

This site has from the 16th through to this century been one of the most important in Deptford's history, having been the base for Trinity House, the East India Company, the General Steam Navigation Company, and a pioneering Power Station.

> **Trinity House** was based here, immediately east of St Nicholas Churchyard, from 1511 (a charter was granted by Henry VIII in 1514) to 1660, when it moved to Water Lane in the City of London; in 1796 it moved to its present building on Tower Hill. The annual Court continued to be held in Deptford until 1852, and Trinity House almshouses remained on the site until 1877. The Corporation of Trinity House was founded as a guild of mariners, to encourage the study of navigation, and to chart the English and Welsh coast. Later it was granted the right to license Thames pilots, to

erect beacons and other navigational aids and structures, and to clear ballast from the river. In 1836 lighthouses throughout England and Wales were transferred to Trinity House; this, and the provision of buoys and beacons, remains its main function today.

The **East India Company** was awarded an exclusive charter in 1600 for 'merchants trading with the East Indies'. It later became the agent of the British Government in India. Many of their ships were built and fitted out here, and at private shipyards nearby. The company moved to Blackwall in 1782, and ceased to exist in 1858.

The **General Steam Navigation Company**, which may have been the world's first commercial steamship company, was founded here 1825. Although they had no dry docks, several of their ships were built here and many others fitted out up to 1970.

Deptford Power Station, the world's first electric power station to generate at high tension for more than just local transmission, was built here by Sebastian de Ferranti for the London Electric Supply Corporation in 1889. It transmitted power to the West End, and from early this century supplied power for tramways and electric trains. In 1926 a new power station (Deptford West) was added to the west. In 1948 a large extension (Deptford East) was built to the original Power Station, making it the second biggest in the country after Barking. The original building was demolished in the late 1960s, Deptford West c1980, and Deptford East finally in 1992.

An old landing stage used by the Power Station, parallel with the riverfront, is visible from Lower Watergate *(see 26B)*. There is a proposal to renovate this in the next few years, and to make it the focus of a community boatyard and the site of a statue of Peter the Great *(see also 28)* to be donated by the Russian Government.

18. Rose Bruford College, Creek Road. This is the Deptford campus of the college of theatre and related arts. It opened here in 1987, in a building of the 1930s which was formerly South East London School.

Rose Bruford (1904-83) was a noted teacher of speech and drama who in 1950 founded the college at Lamorbey House, Sidcup, which is still the main campus.

19. Rachel McMillan Building, a neo-Georgian building of 1930 with a classical doorcase. A plaque states: 'Rachel McMillan College 1930-1977, Margaret McMillan (1860-1931) pioneer of nursery education lived here'. This famous Training College is now the Deptford Campus of the University of Greenwich, housing the School of Environmental Sciences. Behind is the Rachel McMillan Nursery School *(see 22)*.

Margaret McMillan was born in New York in 1860, her sister Rachel in New York 1859. They returned to the home of their maternal grandparents at Inverness in 1865. Margaret took posts as governess and teacher, and became involved in socialist activities. In 1893 she moved to Bradford, and became a founder member of the Independent Labour Party. On election to the Bradford School Board in 1894 she pioneered the medical inspection of schoolchildren. She joined Rachel in London in 1902, living at 51 Tweedy Road Bromley. She campaigned for school meals, and opened school clinics at Deptford Green and at Evelyn Street nearby 1910-11, arranging for children to sleep in the open air. The sisters lived at 127 George Lane, Hither Green, 1910-13. Margaret McMillan opened the nursery school *(see 22)* here 1914, and after the death of Rachel in 1917, it was dedicated to her. She obtained world-wide recognition for her work at the school, and her insistence that nursery teachers needed proper training led to the opening of the Training College in this building in 1930. She became a Companion of Honour in 1930. She died in 1931, and is buried with Rachel at Brockley Cemetery *(see Brockley 18)*.

20. Deptford Methodist Mission, Creek Road. The left half of this large building was reconstructed 1956 after war damage, the right half with its fine corner octagonal dome is of 1903 (a similar dome was on the left corner).

21. The Harp of Erin, Creek Road, a large classical pub of 1897, has a harp in a top gable.

DEPTFORD

Gazetteer

Section 'B' DEPTFORD STRAND
(See map on page 26)

22. *Rachel McMillan Nursery School, located behind the old Rachel McMillan College, and on the same site as the open air nursery school opened by Margaret McMillan and her sister Rachel in 1914. *(See also 19.)* The building to the right of the entrance is almost certainly an original nursery school building of 1917.

In the garden is a memorial to Margaret McMillan, a distinctive stone circular column, probably erected 1937 or 1938; its decorated base has a ring of children with linked hands, and animals and plants in bas-relief. It has been attributed to and is in the style of Eric Gill. It is not visible from outside.

If you have a special interest in viewing the memorial, contact Frances Marriott on 0181-692 4041 to request an appointment.

23. **St Nicholas Church. This is a red brick classical church of 1697, with a ragstone tower remaining from the early 14th century.

> This church, the original parish church of Deptford, is closely linked with British naval history. A church has stood on the site since at least the 12th century. The foundations of the tower are 13th century, and the tower itself early 14th century; the entrance to the church was originally through the tower. Apart from the tower (which at that time had a belfry on top), the church was rebuilt in 1697 by a carpenter, Charles Stanton, who also rebuilt St Mary Magdalene Bermondsey. The top stage of the tower was reconstructed in 1904. After war damage, the church was restored and the interior extensively altered, with great skill, by Thomas Ford in 1958.

On the exterior, note the strange Dutch gables on each side ending in scrolls above notional transepts, and the cherubs over several doors. At the east end, which was largely reconstructed in 1958, is a strange small tower, probably c1716, with elegant oval windows and a small cupola. On the north wall is a tablet of 1606 to John Addey, a master shipwright at the Royal Naval Dockyard and one of the benefactors of Addey and Stanhope School *(see New Cross 33).*

It is worthwhile making a special effort to view the **interior*, which has fine woodwork by Grinling Gibbons, and very interesting furnishings and monuments. *(The church is normally open for viewing between 9 and 10 am and between 11 am and 12 pm on Sunday mornings, otherwise contact Rev Graham Corneck on 0181-692 2749.)*

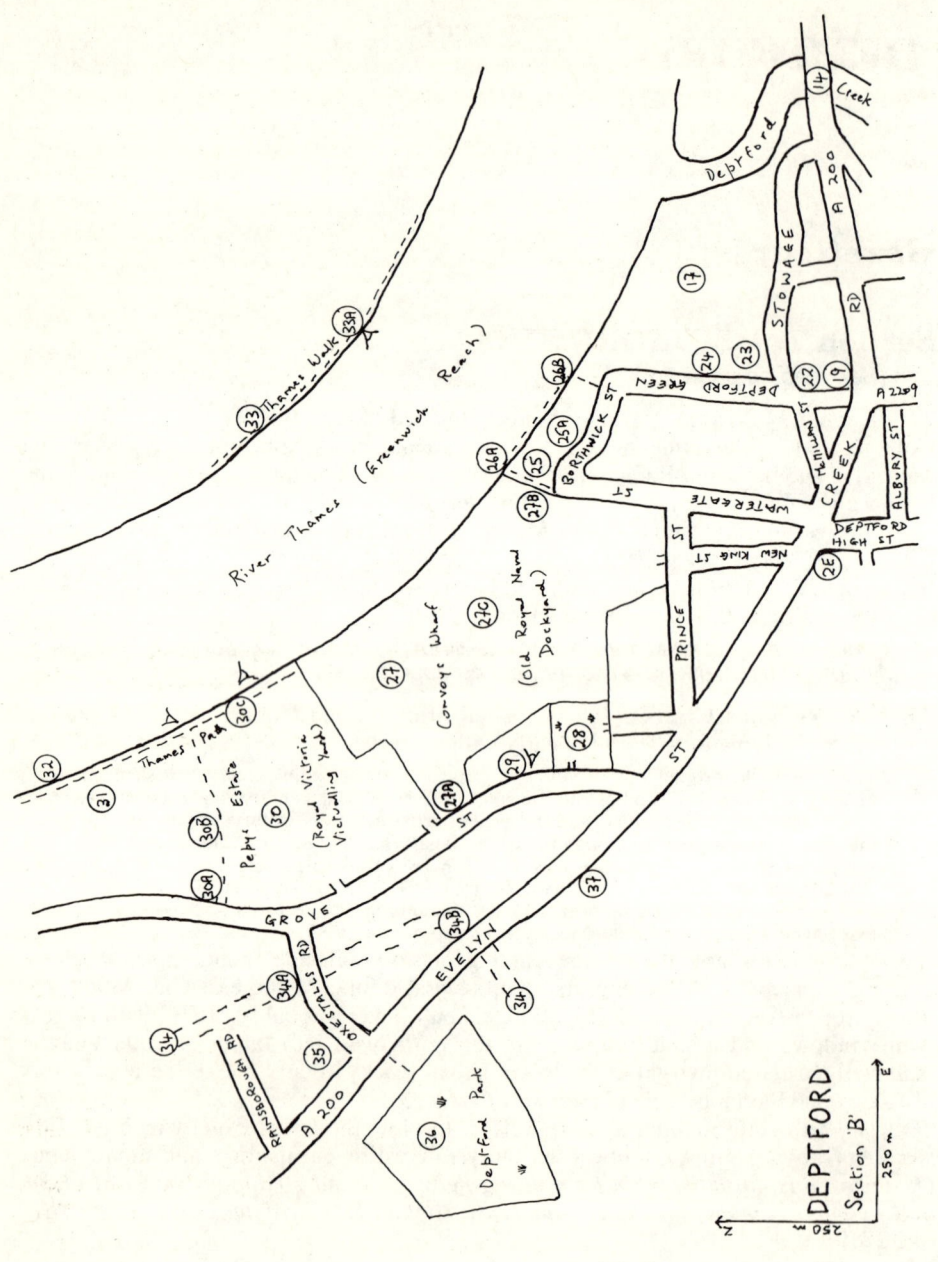

The interior is now almost square, as the former east end was partitioned off for community rooms as part of the 1958 restoration by Thomas Ford. The two eastern columns of the arcade were removed and the reredos repositioned at this point. Four great Tuscan columns (reconstructed in 1958) now remain, and make a square within a square. The large clear glass windows give a light and spacious effect, and this has been enhanced by the removal of the west end gallery in recent years.

The woodwork is mostly of 1697, and is outstanding. Note the magnificent and quite extraordinary oak reredos; it formerly extended three sides around a narrow chancel, but in 1958 was straightened and reduced by one bay to fit its new position along the east wall. The reredos is worth a careful study - note the murals of Moses and Aaron; the pediment containing an illuminated painted oval panel of the Nativity (reconstructed from remains of the chancel window); the coat of arms of William & Mary above; the extensive side panelling curving downwards and embracing elaborately carved doorcases, surmounted by beautiful reclining figures, the one to the right probably Isaiah, the other St John; and lots of other intricate wooden carving. To the right of the reredos is a carved wooden tablet representing Ezekiel's vision in the Valley of the Dry Bones, which used to be over the entrance door to the charnel house in the churchyard *(see below)*. The reredos, and almost certainly the tablet as well, were designed by Grinling Gibbons.

Other fine woodwork includes: a delicately and profusely carved Jacobean pulpit with twisted balusters, supported by a cherub which was formerly a ship's figurehead, c1620 so from an earlier church; a beautiful classical organ case of 1697, with trumpeting angel and cherubs; a Lord's table c1650 and two sanctuary chairs c1720, recently imported.

Note also the modern font designed by Thomas Ford; near the font is an old Bishop's chair, presented by Trinity House in 1958. The three decorative wrought iron tie rods at ceiling level are of 1716. Under the tower archway a modern staircase leads down to the crypt, where large numbers have been buried. A door in the tower gives access to an early 14th century spiral staircase of Purbeck marble.

On the walls are a number of interesting memorials, some extremely well carved, many from the earlier church. Going anti-clockwise from the entrance doorway:

On the south wall, high up near the entrance and difficult to see, a tablet to the shipbuilder Jonas Shish 1680 and family.

On the east wall, at the end of the north aisle, a fine alabaster monument to Roger Boyle 1615 with kneeling figure and skull, resting on top of a tablet to Sir Edward Fenton 1603. Above, a 1730 copy of a painting of Queen Anne by Sir Godfrey Kneller c1713.

On the north wall, an elaborate cartouche to Isaac Loader and other benefactors of the rebuilt church, by Thomas Lucas 1701; and higher up, a tablet to the shipbuilder Peter Pett 1652.

On the west wall, at the end of the north aisle, a tablet to children of the diarist John Evelyn; below, an elegant rounded tablet to Admiral Sir Richard Hughes 1779; and below that, fragments of stone carvings from monuments in the church badly damaged during the last war. Above the tower archway, a copy of the coat of arms of William & Mary 1697. At the end of the south aisle, a 1957 tablet 'to the immortal memory of Christopher Marlowe, who met a tragic death near this spot on the 30th May 1593 ... Cut is the branch that might have grown full straight'.

The dramatist Christopher Marlowe was murdered in Deptford 1593, and was buried in St Nicholas Churchyard, the exact location unknown. The circumstances of his murder have been the subject of considerable controversy. A possible explanation is that he was an agent of Sir Robert Cecil and of Sir Thomas Walsingham, was involved in the campaign to protect Sir Walter Raleigh from the Earl of Essex, and was murdered to ensure his silence.

*Churchyard. The churchyard is enclosed by a tall brick wall, the north and east sides being in part early 17th century. The gate piers are 17th century, and are notable for being topped by skulls (crowned with laurel wreaths) and crossbones (which are 1994 replicas), denoting a burial ground. There are many table tombs, and lots of tablets against the east wall; amongst these is a 1993 tablet inscribed 'Near this spot lie the mortal remains of Christopher Marlowe who met his untimely death in Deptford on 30th May 1593. Cut is the branch that might have grown full straight (Dr Faustus)' *(see above)*.

Forming part of the south wall is a *charnel house (or mortuary), in brick with a high pitched roof, c1701; its interior has been completely altered, and it is sometimes used as a workshop. A wooden tablet, probably by Grinling Gibbons, which was formerly over the entrance door is now in the south aisle of the church *(see above)*.

The churchyard is usually open Friday and Sunday mornings, otherwise contact Rev Graham Corneck on 0181-692 2749

24. St Nicholas House, a large U-shaped block on Deptford Green, was built in 1926 for workers at Deptford Power Station *(see 17)*.

25. Paynes Wharf. This was from c1860 to 1913 the boiler shop of **John Penn & Sons**.

> John Penn & Sons was one of the most important marine engineering firms of the 19th century. In 1825 they started making marine engines at their site at Blackheath Road, Greenwich, and c1860 opened a boilermakers and engine fitting shop here. The firm amalgamated with Thames Ironworks on this site 1899, and ceased production 1913.

Six monumental round-headed arches (probably of the 1860s) facing the river remain from the Penn works; the arches can be seen from the Foreshore Walk *(see below)* when the tide is out.

An iron bollard inscribed 'J. Penn & Son Deptford' rests against the Paynes Wharf wall in Borthwick Street at the junction with Watergate Street.

Paynes Wharf, and the adjoining massive **Borthwick Wharf (25A)**, built as a cold store by Sir Edwin Cooper 1934, both now belong to the Hays Group, which makes no use of the waterfront location.

26. *The Foreshore Walk. When the tide is out, there is a short but fascinating walk along the pebble foreshore in front of Paynes Wharf and Borthwick Wharf. There is access at two points, and the walk can be done in either direction.

Do not attempt the walk along the foreshore unless the tide is out and a broad expanse of pebbles exposed; at other times the strand can be quite treacherous. The steps at Upper Watergate can become very slippery, and extreme care should be taken.

Upper Watergate Stairs (26A), restored c1990, is at the end of a footpath from Watergate Street; note the double line of wooden posts leading into the river, surviving from the causeway of the old Deptford Ferry, a passenger ferry to the Isle of Dogs. **Lower Watergate (26B)**, a drawdock of 1842, slopes down from the east end of Borthwick Street. The walk gives views of the arches of the Penn works *(see above)*, and also of the landing stages, parallel to the riverfront, of the old Deptford Power Station *(see 17)* to the east and of Convoys Wharf *(see 27)* to the west. Burrells Wharf *(see 33A)* can be seen across the river.

27. *Old Royal Naval Dockyard. The site of the old Dockyard is now occupied by **Convoys Wharf**, importers of newsprint, and is surrounded by a (largely modern) brick wall. Most of the buildings are modern, but two adjoining early 18th century buildings and a large part of a covered slipway shed of the 1840s remain. *There is no ready public access to the site, and the views from outside of the older buildings (and indeed of the site as a whole) are highly unsatisfactory - see below.*

> There is evidence of some shipbuilding activity at Deptford in the 15th century. In 1513 Henry VIII set up a naval dockyard, which was called the Kings Yard and became Britain's main dockyard until this role was overtaken at the end of the century by the dockyard at Chatham. It expanded quickly, and was considerably enlarged during the reign of Elizabeth I, leading to an increase in Deptford's population. The dockyard was first enclosed by a brick wall in 1619.
>
> Naval warehouses had been set up at an adjoining site further up-river about the same time as the dockyard. The site was called the Red House by the early 17th century, and in 1742 it became the main Navy Victualling Yard *(see 30)*.
>
> The two sites, though distinct, were naturally closely associated. The dockyard and the area up-river saw the launch of many of the great voyages of discovery, including those of Sir Francis Drake, Sir Martin Frobisher and Sir Walter Raleigh, and (two centuries later) Captain James Cook and Captain George Vancouver.
>
> The dockyard continued to be enlarged during the 17th and 18th centuries, but Chatham (set up c1570) had been expanding much faster, and nearby Woolwich (set up 1512) was also expanding.
>
> In 1822 the first successful naval steamship was launched at Deptford, but the engines had been made elsewhere. Deptford was not a suitable site for setting up a steam factory, nor for making and (because the river was too shallow) launching the iron ships now required. In 1830 shipbuilding stopped; but breaking up of old ships continued and refits of steamships started, and the yard was reopened in 1844 for building wooden ships covered with iron plates.
>
> From 1862 Chatham dockyard was greatly expanded, and this led to the final closure of both Deptford and Woolwich in 1869, causing immense distress throughout the area. Over 450 ships had been built at Deptford, and many others repaired.
>
> The Corporation of London opened most of the site as a foreign cattle market in 1871. The docks and basins were filled in and many of the old buildings demolished. A siding from the freight railway to Deptford Wharf operated into the site between 1900 and 1932. The cattle market closed 1912, and the site became a supply depot in the first world war. It remained in War Department control until after the last war, though many other users (including Convoys) had come onto the site.
>
> Convoys Ltd purchased the entire site in 1984, and it is now called Convoys Wharf, containing mainly warehousing used for the import of newsprint. It is now probably the largest working wharf in Inner London.

The entrance to the Dockyard site is in Prince Street. An additional entrance was opened in Grove Street in the 19th century, probably c1871 after the cattle market was set up, and from this time two square brick gate piers topped by ball finials **(27A)** have survived; this entrance was bricked up in 1993. The rail siding from the Deptford Wharf line entered the site just to the left, and at this point there is now a gate of 1993 which is usually closed but is sometimes used by Convoys.

The site contains a mass of buildings and structures. The following are of special interest:

*Master Shipwright's House (27B), now known as Nelson House, an impressive (though derelict) brick building of 1708 by the eastern boundary wall, facing west into the site. It has twin roofs; there were originally five dormers on both front and rear, but one of the front ones has not survived. Around the modern front door is evidence of a disappeared doorcase. The north front, facing the river, has been painted white; it has lost its gable and so looks oddly truncated. Adjoining the north front is a single storey extension, probably c1710, with a finely decorated early 19th century porch; it is linked to a two storey outhouse, probably early 19th century, reaching right to the boundary wall.

Adjoining to the south and also facing west into the site is the ***Naval Office**, now known as Hamilton House, also derelict, probably c1700. Though somewhat lower than the Master Shipwright's House, the two buildings make an impressive pair; both are of brown brick with red brick dressings. Note the giant pilasters at either end, and the mansard roof; the dormers and the doors are modern. The two buildings originally formed part of a longer terrace.

*The covered slipways (27C), now called Olympia. This is part of a massive iron-framed shed of 1848, with great swooping twin corrugated roofs which originally covered two slipways. It is now stranded in the middle of the site, as the eastern section which extended to the riverfront has been removed, as have glazed strips which ran along the top.

Near Olympia is an impressive tall round water tank of 1987.

The Convoys office building with a gabled side facing the Prince Street entrance is late 19th century.

Several short sections of railway track from the siding which was linked to the Deptford Wharf branch between 1900 and 1932 have survived, as well as sections of narrow gauge railway used within the site from the early 1930s.

Along the riverfront is a long concrete landing stage constructed in 1934 by the Danish firm of Christiani & Nielsen, which had pioneered the use of reinforced concrete. It was linked to the bank by three bridges, but it has recently been strengthened and is now linked by four bridges. There is also to the west a roll-on roll-off terminal of 1976 projecting slightly further into the river. The river frontage is now dominated by three striking large modern buildings - going up-river, a grey shed of 1984, a green shed of 1987, and a green shed of 1993.

> *The site is closed to the public. If you have a special interest in viewing the buildings on the site, write to the Managing Director, Convoys Wharf, Prince Street, London SE8 3JH. For safety reasons, because of the nature of the work conducted on the site, all visitors have to be accompanied by an official.*

Views from outside into the site are not very rewarding. In Watergate Street, near the junction with Borthwick Street, it is possible to see over the wall the upper part of the rear of the Master Shipwright's House and of the adjoining Naval Offices; at this point there is a section of 18th century wall, with two adjacent piers projecting above the wall coping. From various points on the western side, best of all from outside the Princess of Wales pub *(see 29)*, there are tantalising glimpses of the top of the covered slipways and of the modern water tank. The Convoys office building can be seen clearly from the Prince Street entrance. The Thames Walk on the Isle of Dogs *(see 33)* provides a fine view of the white north front of the Master Shipwright's House, of the three modern riverfront sheds and the landing-stage.

Note also that the clock tower and belfry of 1762 from the Great Storehouse (demolished 1981) were in 1987 placed on top of a modern tower in the main shopping centre at Thamesmead Central.

28. Sayes Court Park. This park is of great historical interest as the only remaining identifiable part of the grounds of Sayes Court.

> Sayes Court was the manor house of Deptford, and the first building dated back at least to the 12th century. The diarist John Evelyn lived there from 1652 to 1694, and enlarged and partly rebuilt it. Peter the Great was a tenant for several months in early 1698, while he was studying shipbuilding at the Dockyard, and the damage done to the property during his stay is notorious. Sayes Court was demolished and rebuilt in 1729, becoming a workhouse and then almshouses, and part of the site was laid out as a recreation ground in 1878. Much of the grounds was absorbed into the Dockyard in 1927. The building was finally demolished c1930; its site, opposite the end of Czar Street, is now within the Dockyard area.

The present park occupies only a small area in the western part of the former grounds. The mulberry tree in the centre is said to be from a cutting of a mulberry tree dating back to Evelyn's time. The symbolic gates at the entrance from Sayes Court Street, off Prince Street, were designed by Annalisa Colombara and installed 1997.

29. Princess of Wales, 88 Grove Street. A pub of 1883 with lots of decorative flourishes. The best view of the covered slipways in the Dockyard site *(see 27C)* is from Barnes Terrace nearby.

30. Pepys Estate. This vast estate was built by the London County Council and Greater London Council 1961-69, and extended c1980. It is notable for having successfully incorporated several Georgian buildings remaining from the ****Royal Victoria Victualling Yard.**

> Naval warehouses had been set up about the same time as the dockyard at an adjoining site further up-river. The site was called the Red House by the early 17th century, and in 1742 it became the main Navy Victualling Depot. The name of the yard was changed to Royal Victoria Victualling Yard after Queen Victoria's visit in 1858. It stored clothing, rum, meat and other foodstuffs for the Navy, and also manufactured biscuits, chocolate, and mustard. It closed in 1961, thus out-lasting the Dockyard by nearly 100 years. *See also 27.*

The three tower blocks (two clad in gleaming white steel, the other due to be similarly clad in 1998) form a stark contrast to the long and restless dark brick slab blocks of the estate, as well as to the stock brick buildings of the Victualling Yard. Note also the youth club and social club, two buildings with sharply pointed oasthouse-like roofs on Grove Street near the small shopping centre. The remaining buildings of the Victualling Yard have been handsomely converted:

The ***gateway (30A)**, of 1788, consists of two ornamental white stone arches linked by an iron lampholder. Over each arch is an ox skull and garlands, and a hollowed medallion with intertwined anchors. In front are four genuine late 18th century cannon used as bollards, and also to the left an unusual Turnpike Property Mark of 1855 (the only such mark to survive), inscribed 'This land is part of the Bermondsey, Rotherhithe & Deptford Turnpike Roads'.

Adjoining the gateway is the ***Colonnade Building**, of 1788, consisting of two houses linked by a front colonnade of 19 Doric columns.

Beyond is *****The Terrace (30B)**, of the 1780s, a symmetrical and attractive composition of seven houses; the centre and end houses are pedimented and project slightly.

On the riverside walk is *****Foreshore (30C)**, two long and attractive terraces of the 1780s. They are former warehouses, each ending in a projecting pavilion with fine fanlights, facing each other in the centre. The pavilion to the right was the superintendent's house, and the one to the left the administration offices. Each warehouse is arcaded with great timber pillars along the ground floor. Rum was stored in the warehouse to the left. Go between the two blocks, and on the right are the former **stables**, probably contemporary.

On the river in front of the warehouses is a gate leading to *****Drake's Steps**, also known as the Queen's Stairs, much restored but very impressive. A nearby plaque commemorates the knighting of Sir Francis Drake by Elizabeth I on the 'Golden Hind' in 1581 after his round the world voyage; this took place on the Deptford waterfront, but it is not known exactly where.

Two vermiculated piers, which once framed the Queen's Stairs, can be seen on the *****Thames Path**, here called Deptford Strand; there are also old hoists and several old cannon. The riverside walk runs from the Dockyard wall alongside the Pepys Estate to Deptford Wharf, then on into Surrey Docks. The views extend from Canary Wharf round to Greenwich. On the Isle of Dogs opposite, Cyclops Wharf of 1991 is directly ahead, and the smaller Phoenix Court of 1992 is to the right, both being in Docklands vernacular style; Burrells Wharf *(see 33A)* is further to the right.

31. Deptford Wharf. This housing development, completed 1992, has a formal classical layout and is in Docklands post-modernist style. It was built on the site of a fan of railway sidings and docks called Deptford Wharf.

> The Deptford Wharf branch was a freight line (carrying mainly coal) to the Croydon Railway at New Cross Gate and to the South London Line at Peckham between 1849 and 1963. Part of the old railway embankment can be seen at Rainsborough Avenue going eastwards from Evelyn Street to the old route of the Grand Surrey Canal *(see 34)*. From the Wharf a siding ran along Grove Street and into the Foreign Cattle Market from 1900 to 1932 *(see 27)*.

The **Thames Path** here continues the walk on the Pepys Estate *(see above)* and provides similar Docklands views.

32. St Georges Stairs, an old river access point; the stairs were modernised in 1987. At low tide timbers said to be from a 17th century slipway are exposed, as well as the concrete covered outlet of the Earl Sluice, which is now culverted.

Beyond, on the riverside walk, is a Portland stone pier which was a parish **boundary stone** of 1819, linked by a low brick wall sloping down to a similar pier to the left. The right-hand pier is inscribed SPD (St Pauls Deptford) 1819 and SMR (St Mary Rotherhithe) 1819, also 1877 and 1886 (the later dates being when the boundary was ratified). The stone was relocated here 1988 from a position on a former bridge nearby over the Earl Sluice, which formed the actual parish boundary, and was in fact the boundary between Kent and Surrey before 1889 (when the London County Council was formed).

33. *Thames Walk, Millwall, Isle of Dogs. This riverside walk behind Westferry Road at the south-west tip of the Isle of Dogs provides wonderful *****views** of the Deptford Waterfront. From left to right, clearly visible are: the mouth of Deptford

**St Paul's Church
(Thomas Archer, 1713-23)**
- *Deptford 3*

**Albury Street, north side
(Thomas Lucas, 1706-17)**
- *Deptford 4*

19/31 Tanners Hill (c1690) - *Deptford 7*

13 Deptford High Street (1838) & Deptford Market - *Deptford 2*

St Nicholas Church (1697, tower early 14th century) & charnel house (c1701) - *Deptford 23*

Paynes Wharf (probably 1860's) - *Deptford 25*

Master Shipwright's House (1708) & Naval Office (c1700) - *Deptford 27B*

Covered slipways, Old Royal Naval Dockyard (1848) - *Deptford 27C*

Gateway & Colonnade (1788), Royal Victoria Victualling Yard - *Deptford 30A*

Foreshore (1780s), Royal Victoria Victualling Yard - *Deptford 30C*

**St Johns Church
(Philip Charles
Hardwick, 1854)**
- *Deptford 47*

**88/134 Albyn Road
(late 1850s)**
- *Deptford 39A*

Stone House (George Gibson, 1773) - *Deptford 46*

Stone House portico (George Gibson, 1773) - *Deptford 46*

207/219 New Cross Road (1841) - *New Cross 2A*

Deptford Town Hall (Lanchester & Rickards, 1905) - *New Cross 27*

Goldsmiths College (John Shaw, 1844) - *New Cross 28*

Laurie Grove Baths (Thomas Dinwiddy, 1898) - *New Cross 28A*

**Addey & Stanhope School
(Sir Alfred Brunwell Thomas, 1899)** - *New Cross 33*

Zion Chapel (1876)
- *New Cross 35*

**St Peters Church
(Frederick Marrable 1868,
Sir Arthur Blomfield 1891)**
- *Brockley 8*

Glensdale Road, north side (c1878) - *Brockley 7*

133/5 Breakspears Road (1880) - *Brockley 9*

98 Tressillian Road (c1879) - *Brockley 10*

Prendergast School (1885) - *Brockley 12A*

Brockley Jack (1898) - *Brockley 21*

Clock Tower (1897) & old Co-op Store (1933) - *Lewisham 9, 15*

The Old Station (1871) - *Lewisham 31*

St Saviours Church (1909), campanile & presbytery (1929)
- Lewisham 17

78 Lewisham Park (c1860)
- Lewisham 57A

Church of St Mary the Virgin (George Gibson, 1777) - *Lewisham 63*

Ladywell House (1693) - *Lewisham 48*

Creek; the Stowage site, with the old Power Station landing stage parallel with the bank; the bulky Borthwick Wharf of 1934; Paynes Wharf with the great round arches of the old John Penn works, probably of the 1860s; the white north front of the Master Shipwright's House of 1708, just within the Old Dockyard site; the three great modern sheds of Convoys Wharf, of 1984, 1987 and 1993 - there may well be ships alongside the great concrete landing-stage of 1934 and the roll-on roll-off terminal of 1976; the Foreshore buildings of the Victualling Yard, of the 1780s; and the Aragon Tower of the postwar Pepys Estate. Further to the right is the Deptford Wharf estate.

A good place along the Thames Walk from which to appreciate these views is **Burrells Wharf (33A)**, which is of outstanding interest in its own right. It is an attractive housing development designed by Jestico & Whiles 1990 on an industrial site of great historical importance.

> The wharf was laid out by William Fairbairn in 1836, the first large-scale purpose-built commercial yard for building iron ships in the country. From 1853-57 the Great Eastern, designed by Isambard Kingdom Brunel, by far the largest ship built between 1850 and 1900 and the largest ever to be built on the Thames, was constructed here, and eventually (after many unsuccessful attempts) launched here in 1858. It was however not successful or economical, and it was broken up at Birkenhead 1891. In the 1860s the site became Millwall Ironworks, and from 1888 to 1986 Burrells Paint and Colour Works.
>
> The development incorporates several converted 19th century buildings, but two buildings on the main square which are still clearly recognisable as industrial buildings are of special interest - the Plate House, Italianate of 1853, where steel plate was made for the Great Eastern, now well converted to a leisure centre; and the Ironworks chimney of the 1860s, not so tall as the original, now providing district heating for the complex.
>
> The wooden piles and cross-pieces exposed to the north of the complex are thought to be the remains of the launching-pad of the ship.

34. Grand Surrey Canal. The route of the canal, which closed in 1971 and is now completely filled in, can be readily identified from two bridges in this area - the **Oxestalls Road Bridge (34A)**, built for the Pepys Estate in the 1960s (the canal route to the north is now covered by an embankment); and **Blackhorse Bridge (34B)**, Evelyn Street, an iron girder bridge of 1888. *(See also New Cross 11.)*

> The Grand Surrey Canal was an ambitious concept of Ralph Dodd which was planned to link the Surrey Docks with Kingston and Epsom. It was begun in 1802, and by 1807 it had reached a point in New Cross from which the Croydon Canal was constructed, reaching Croydon in 1809. By 1811 the Surrey Canal had only reached Camberwell, a distance of under 5 kilometres. A branch from Camberwell to Peckham was opened in 1826. Transport of timber was always the main use, and in later days there were extensive timber yards along its banks.

35. Deptford Park School, a prominent London School Board building c1884.

36. Deptford Park, a large open space, opened 1897. It is rather bare, though there are rows of fine plane trees around all four sides.

37. St Lukes Church, Evelyn Street, a ragstone Gothic church of 1872, with an apsed chancel and a stumpy tower. The interior has been partitioned for community organisations, leaving only a small area around the old chancel for the church.

It forms an interesting group with, to the right, **Deptford Fire Station**, a handsome Queen Anne style red brick building of 1903; and to the left **192 Evelyn Street**, a tall house, probably of the 1830s.

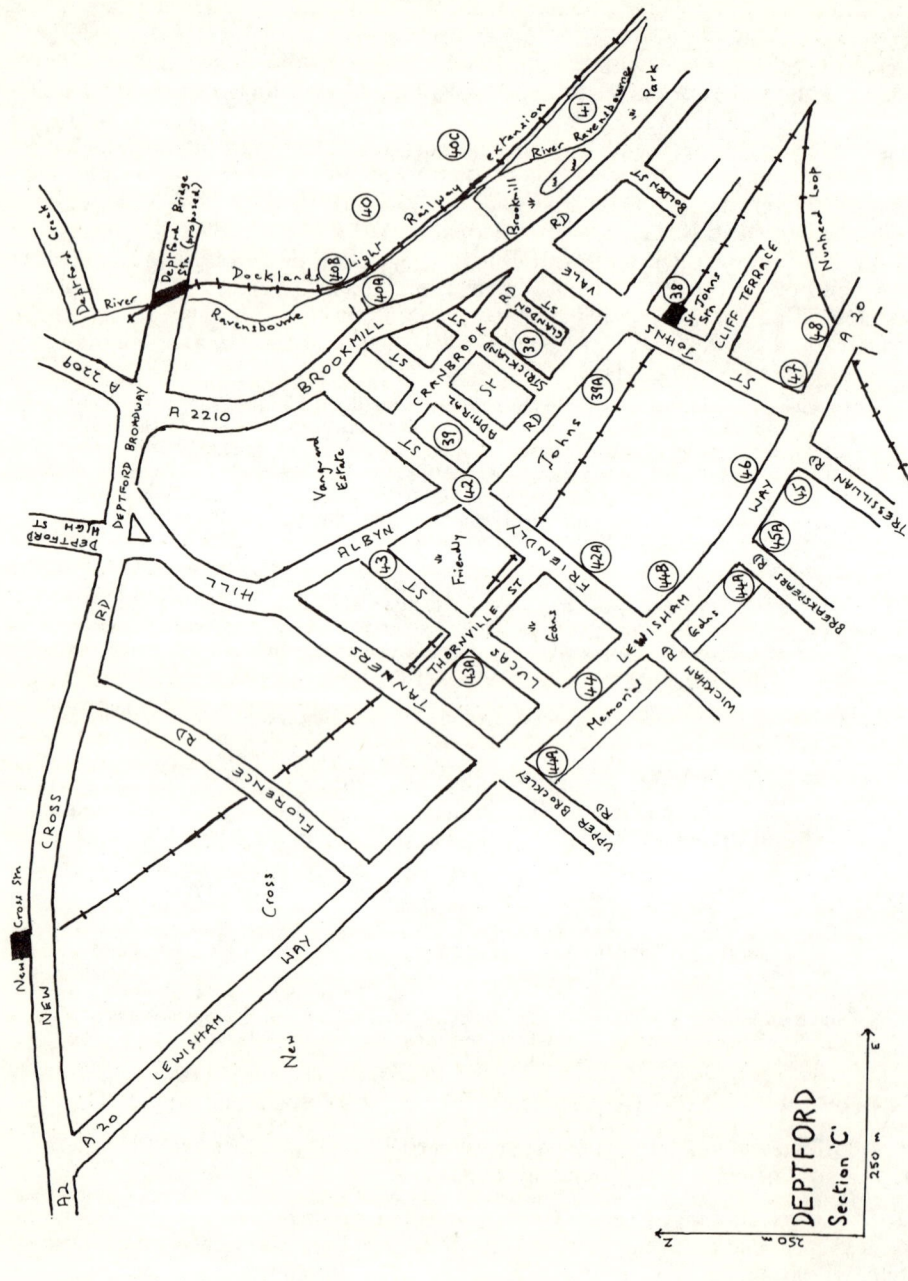

DEPTFORD

Gazetteer

Section 'C' NEW TOWN & ST JOHNS

38. St Johns Station, opened 1873, has no proper station building. A pedestrian bridge leads down to the platforms, on which the present structures are of 1983. The bridge in St Johns Vale gives fine views on both sides of the large number of tracks - note the higher level track skirting the station to the south, opened 1976. Note also the late Victorian wall letter-box set into the wall on the southern side of the bridge.

39. St Johns. The area to the east of Friendly Street is nowadays commonly known as St Johns. The section north of the railway line, built between 1855 and 1875, is the best preserved part of Deptford New Town. **Albyn Road** is the pivotal street; in this and nearby streets are a number of well preserved terraces and groups, generally of a high standard of design.

*__*88/134 Albyn Road (39A)__*, on the south side, are the most attractive in the area - there are groups of two, four and six houses, all with fine cornices; the end houses have graceful full-height shallow bows, the middle ones ornamental bracketed hoods over paired doorways. (Note that no 88 is a modern rebuild.) In the terraces opposite, the end houses have full-height canted bays. All these houses, between Admiral Street and St Johns Vale, are of the late 1850s.

Groups of houses in nearby streets also have many end houses with full-height bows or canted bays - **Admiral Street**, of the early 1860s; **Strickland Street**, of the mid 1860s; **Cranbrook Road** and **St Johns Vale**, of the 1860s and early 1870s. But they do not show the same consistent pattern, nor do they have quite the appeal of the houses in Albyn Road. Note also **The Cranbrook,** a pub at the end of Cranbrook Street, and **Clandon Street**, a close off Cranbrook Road, both of the early 1870s. There are also much larger houses, of the late 1860s, beyond the railway in St Johns Vale and in nearby **Cliff Terrace**, where one house shows Gothic influences.

Further east, at **16 Bolden Street (39B)**, a house of the 1870s, is a Lewisham Council plaque: 'Thankfull Sturdee 1852-1934, local historian and photographer, lived here 1900-1903'. He was known as the father of Fleet Street photography, and is now mainly remembered for his 'Reminiscences of Old Deptford' (1895).

40. Deptford Pumping Station, of Thames Water Utilities, is the oldest surviving industrial installation in Deptford. The site is closed to the public, but there are views from outside of the major buildings on the site.

> Ravensbourne Water Company was founded here in 1701, water being taken direct from the Ravensbourne. It became Kent Waterworks in 1809; three wells - known as Coldbath, Garden, and The Twins - were sunk about 30 metres into the chalk between 1849 and 1876, and water was not taken from the river after 1862. The Metropolitan Water Board took over in 1903, and sunk a new main well 40 metres deep in 1930, connected by adits or underground passages to the older wells. All these wells are still in use, and supply water to a large area of South East London. (The capped tops of the Coldbath and Garden wells are readily visible outside the site - *see 41.*) The site will be bisected by the Docklands Light Railway.

Two mid 19th century buildings (though much altered) have survived on the site, and are visible from the entrance in Brookmill Road.

To the right is the old **Kent Waterworks head office and manager's house (40A)**. It is now the regional office of London Water Supply, but this use may cease with the coming of the Docklands Light Railway.

Straight ahead is the **Cornish Engine House (40B)**, the only 19th century engine house remaining. The central two sections are c1850; the sections on either side are also basically mid 19th century, but the one to the left was altered c1922 and the one to the right c1936; both alterations, though substantial, are in a sympathetic style. It ceased use as an engine house in 1932, and is now used for storage. The view from Brookmill Road is likely to be partly obstructed by the Docklands Light Railway.

The dominant building on the site is the former **Main Engine House (40C)** of 1932, a large red brick building, best viewed from Brookmill Park *(see below)*. The engines have gone, but it still contains the main well, connected by adits to the other three wells, as well as three well pumps of 1995. The new Pump House and other modern installations of 1995 are not visible from outside the site.

> *There is no ready public access to the site. If you have a special interest in viewing the site, write to Customer Centre, Thames Water, Walnut Court, Swindon SN2 6FN.*

41. Brookmill Park, formerly called Ravensbourne Park, opened 1953. It occupies part of the former grounds of Deptford Pumping Station; the Main Engine House of 1932 is clearly visible from the Park. It is an attractive park, with a lake, and views of the river, at present not particularly appealing in its concrete channel. The lake once formed part of a large reservoir, twice the size of the lake. Within a stone enclosure in the southern part is the capped top of the Garden Well of 1863; the well below is connected by an adit to the main well in the Pumping Station. *(See also 40.)*

However, the construction of the Docklands Light Railway will transform the appearance of the park, as the river will be re-routed and its banks landscaped, and the railway will run along the present river bed. During the construction period to 1999, there will inevitably be considerable disruption.

A pedestrian bridge over the river leads to the Coldbath Estate; the Elverson Road Station of the Docklands Light Railway will be constructed near this point. The capped top of the Coldbath Well of 1859, also connected by an adit to the main well in the Pumping Station, is now in the grounds of Servite House, Coldbath Street; it can be seen clearly from the Estate.

To the south of the park is an abandoned railway embankment on both sides of Brookmill Road; it was on the Greenwich Park Line between the former Blackheath Hill and Lewisham Road Stations *(see Lewisham 31)*. It is now **Brookmill Nature Reserve**, a wildlife site, but with no ready access for the public.

42. Friendly Street. Terraces survive only on the east side. Two terraces to the south, **nos 12/16** and **18/26 (42A)**, are of 1806, though much restored; the houses are double-fronted and well-designed. The terraces north of Albyn Road have smaller houses, of 1844 as far as Cranbrook Road, and of 1847 beyond, including the pub **The Crown and Sceptre**. On the west side is the **Vanguard Estate**, a Peabody estate of the 1970s, with mostly weatherboarded upper floors.

43. Lucas Street retains two rows of cottages, and the adjoining part of **Albyn Road** two short terraces, of the early 1840s (though some are postwar rebuilds).

Note also **Lucas Vale School (43A)**, a bulky building of 1885, with an extraordinary two storey oriel.

44. Lewisham Way. This road leads from New Cross, and after crossing the Nunhead Loop railway joins Loampit Hill on its way to the Lewisham town centre. The road has numerous groups of fine 19th century houses, as well as several individual buildings of great interest, including Goldsmiths College, Deptford Library, Stone House, Lewisham College, St Johns Church.

Only the eastern part of Lewisham Way is featured here. For the western part, from the Marquis of Granby to Upper Brockley Road / Tanners Hill, including Goldsmiths College and Deptford Library, see New Cross 28-31.

The even numbers are on the south side, the odd numbers on the north side. Going from west to east:

The Memorial Gardens (44A) stretch from Upper Brockley Road to Breakspears Road, with Wickham Road breaking through. They were originally private enclosed gardens for the residents of **Wickham Terrace**, a group of 25 large and impressive houses, built behind the gardens 1849-55. The gardens were bought by Deptford Council 1924; at the Upper Brockley Road end is the **Deptford War Memorial** of 1921, a large and handsome octagonal column.

In the central part of Wickham Terrace, 14 houses have survived, and are flanked by postwar houses which are more or less successful pastiches of the original.

At the western end **no 158**, a large block of c1968, on the site of the demolished Brockley Congregational Church, is a not so successful pastiche aiming to look like two large houses. Between Manor Avenue and Wickham Road are the surviving original houses - **nos 160/6**, linked pairs of 1852; **no 168**, detached and attractive, of 1852; **nos 170/184**, linked pairs of the early 1850s; and **York House**, no 186, very attractive, of 1849. Beyond Wickham Road a group of four large buildings (three linked to form a terrace) are currently (in 1997) under construction and will be more successful pastiches of the originals.

Nos 225/235, a terrace of cottages of 1838, formerly called Victoria Cottages.

For Lewisham College and Lea House, see 45.

No 239, large and florid, of brick and terracotta with ornamented gables and pinnacles, designed 1886 by James Edmeston for London & South Western Bank.

Nos **239a/241, 243a/245** and **247a/249 (44B)** are three stuccoed pairs of 1806 with shared pedimented gables covering the entire width of the building. Originally known as **Brunswick Place**, they are in the striking individual style (of which there are many examples in the Blackheath area) considered as influenced by the architect Michael Searles. In 1885 shops were built out in front, and the coach-houses were replaced by taller and very fanciful brick buildings with gables linked by curved sections, thus forming a terrace of a very intriguing pattern. No 249a is a surviving coach-house for no 249, but altered and enlarged.

Nos 251/3, a substantial pair of 1866 with fine ornamentation.

Nos 255/265, a terrace of attractive tall houses of 1867 decorated with wreaths.

For Stone House, see 46.

Nos 283/5, a pair of 1868, with large bows through two storeys and basement.

For St Johns Church, see 47. For the Welsh Presbyterian Church, see 48.

Nos 228/230 & 232/4 are pairs c1871, and showing Gothic influence. **Nos 236/8** is a handsome Italianate pair of 1858.

45. Lewisham College (of Further Education), an associate college of the University of Greenwich, before 1990 known as SELTEC (South East London Technical College). There are 11,000 students. *(See also 8A.)*

The main building is **Tressillian Building**, a long rectangular brick block with rows of close tall windows, built 1931. Note the decorative plaques, the two great coats of arms (London County Council and Metropolitan Borough of Deptford) above the entrance, and finely designed arts and crafts lamp-posts and rainwater heads.

Next door is ***Lea House (45A)**, 210/212 Lewisham Way, a fine stuccoed Italianate pair, of 1853. Behind is **Breakspears Building**, on Breakspears Road, a brutalist block of 1977, looking much like a multi-storey car park.

46. **Stone House, 281 Lewisham Way. This villa was built for himself 1771-73 by George Gibson. It is quite an extraordinary phenomenon - it was in fact called Comical House in the mid 19th century. In the centre of each side is a full height bow, except to the west where a grand staircase leads directly up to a grand portico at first floor level, and the bow is at this level only. The main ground floor entrance is in the bow on the east side.

The house is of ragstone with stone bands, window surrounds and quoins. The ground floor has at each corner thick buttresses curved out at the base. The windows and doors are square-headed at ground floor level, and round-headed at first floor level (including three in each bow). The bow to the north was extended outwards in the late 19th century. The portico has six great columns with unusual capitals of leaves and flowers (similar to the capitals in the portico of St Marys Lewisham, *see Lewisham 63*); above is a large pediment and a short classical frieze. On the roof is an attic floor behind a concave curved parapet, and a glazed cupola which is not visible from outside.

The ***interior** is also remarkable, the bows allowing for a sequence of circular rooms (some with curved doors) around the central stairwell. The entrance in the east face leads to a circular vestibule, which leads to the stairwell. To the right is a saloon, oval because of the extended bow, with a fine classical fireplace and murals of Greenwich and St Pauls Cathedral by Peter Kent 1994. The stairwell is octagonal, four sides being recessed, and at an upper level are roundels with busts in bas-relief of Hanoverian kings; it is top-lit by the cupola, and at the attic level is surrounded by a balustrade. In the cupola is a bell dated 1766.

On the first floor, the drawing room faces west into the portico, and is tripartite - the central room is circular, and has a fine marble fireplace and domed painted ceiling (both probably c1830), and Ionic pilasters around the wall; on either side, part separated by Ionic columns, are square rooms with vaulted ceilings. The room to the north of the drawing-room is oval, and has a frieze; the room to the south is circular and has a fine classical fireplace and frieze.

To the west of Stone House is a long modern brick wall inset with blind stone doorways from demolished houses, 267/279 Lewisham Way, which were built in 1867 on the garden of Stone House; it now forms the rear garden wall of the postwar Ashmead School.

> Stone House and its grounds are privately owned and are not open to the public. The views from outside are not very satisfactory, except perhaps for the east and south sides, which can be viewed from the entrance. There is a view of the north side from a yard at the top of St Johns Vale; and of the portico on the west side over the wall along Lewisham Way.

47. *****St Johns Church**, a Gothic ragstone church of 1854 by Philip Charles Hardwick. Its very tall broach spire is a landmark for a long way around. Note the entrance arch with foliated capitals and dogtooth ornamentation, and the large west window.

The *****interior** *(contact the vicarage in the churchyard, or ring 0181-692 2857)* is imposing - note the very high chancel arch, the intricately carved stone reredos like a screen, original pews, later galleries over the aisles, the large stone pulpit of 1903, the colourful east window, and on the west wall of the south aisle the John Allen monument of 1865. The west window (by Ward & Hughes) is glorious, but can no longer be seen from the church, as a postwar hall has been erected across the upper part of the church at the west end, and it can only be seen from inside the hall.

48. Presbyterian Church of Wales, 289 Lewisham Way. The part to the left is the church of 1924, of dark brick and rather uninspired. The part to the right is more interesting - it is the former Lucas Villa of 1823, built for Jonathan Lucas, the major landholder of Deptford New Town; it has great bow windows on either side of the entrance. It was the Vicarage of St Johns from 1854 to 1924, and is now the vicarage of the Welsh Presbyterian Church.

DEPTFORD

Suggested Walks

It is recommended that the suggested walks be followed in conjunction with the Gazetteer and the maps, and that the Gazetteer be consulted at each location for a detailed description. Most locations described in the Gazetteer are covered; some other locations have not been included, as they might add too much to the length of the walks.

Walk no 1 covers Section 'A', Walk no 2 Section 'B', and Walk no 3 Section 'C'. The walks follow a more or less circular route, so can be joined at any location. Walks nos 1 & 2 begin and end at Deptford Station, and Walk no 3 at St Johns Station.

WALK no 1 (including Deptford Station, Deptford High Street, Albury Street, St Pauls Church, Deptford Broadway, Deptford Bridge, Creekside, Deptford Creek Bridge, Stowage). Distance approx 4 kilometres.

NB. This walk is best undertaken on Wednesday, Friday or Saturday afternoons, when St Pauls Church is normally open, and Deptford Market is in operation (though this can make it rather difficult to move around the southern end of Depfford High Street). However, the interior of Our Lady of the Assumption Church is unlikely to be open at these times, unless a prior arrangement has been made.

On leaving **Deptford Station (1),** turn left along **Deptford High Street (2)**. The best way to see the most interesting buildings and other features is to proceed block by block, as in the gazetteer. First the block from the railway bridge northwards to Albury Street **(2A)**, and then the block continuing northwards to the end of the High Street **(2B)**. If you have time, see also the buildings in **Clyde Street (2C)** and in **Lamerton Street (2D)**.

Retrace steps along the High Street, and turn left along **Albury Street (4)**. At the end turn right into Deptford Church Street, and right again into the **churchyard** of **St Pauls Church (3)**. If the church is open, view the interior.

Return to the High Street, and turn left back to the railway bridge. Immediately past the Station, turn left for a look along **Mechanics Path (1B)**, return, cross the road and proceed ahead into the station yard to see the **ramp (1A)**. Back in the High Street, note **Our Lady of the Assumption Church (5)**; try to see the interior. Then continue southwards along the High Street, first the block to Douglas Way / Giffin Street **(2F)**, then divert along Douglas Way to **The Albany (2H)** and retrace steps, then walk along the block to the end of the High Street at Deptford Broadway **(2G)**.

On reaching the Broadway, cross the road to **Tanners Hill,** and note **nos 13/31 (7)** on the left. Return to **Deptford Broadway (8)** and look at the buildings all around. Turn right down Brookmill Road to **Mereton Mansions (9)** and **Sylva Cottages (9A)**. Return to the Broadway and turn right onto **Deptford Bridge (10)**, then return and turn right down Deptford Church Street.

Continue along Church Street, noting **nos 1/11** opposite, until you reach **The Birds Nest (11)**, then turn right down **Creekside (13)**. Note the **railway viaduct (12B)** on both sides of the road, and then the mural **Love Over Gold (13B)**. Continue, turn right down **Copperas Street**, and right for **Deptford Creek Bridge (14)**. Cross the road and proceed westwards back along Creek Road.

Pass **The Hoy Inn (15)** and **The Duke (16)**, and look down Gonson Street; the **Stowage** site **(17)** is directly ahead. Continue along Creek Road, noting on the south side **Rose Bruford College (18)**, and on the north side the **Rachel McMillan Building (19)**, **Deptford Methodist Mission (20)**, and **The Harp of Erin (21)**. Cross the road to **The Noahs Ark (2E)**, turn down Deptford High Street, and you are soon back at Deptford Station.

WALK no 2 (including St Nicholas Church, the former Royal Naval Dockyard and Royal Victoria Victualling Yard sites, and part of the route of the Grand Surrey Canal). Distance approx 4 kilometres.

> *NB. This walk is best undertaken on Friday or Sunday mornings, when St Nicholas Churchyard is normally open. If you can make an advance arrangement to view the interior - see the gazetteer- so much the better.*

On leaving **Deptford Station (1)**, turn left along **Deptford High Street (2)**, walk to the end and cross the road. Bear right along McMillan Street; at the end is **Rachel McMillan Nursery School (22)**. Bear left to the gates of the **churchyard** of St **Nicholas Church (23)**, on Deptford Green. If the gates are open, walk around the church exterior, see the **Charnel House**, and try to view the church interior.

Continue along Deptford Green, passing **St Nicholas House (24)**, and bear left into Borthwick Street; on the right **Lower Watergate (26C)** leads down to the river. Only if the tide is right out (see the gazetteer), take the **Foreshore Walk (26)** past the great round-headed arches of **Paynes Wharf (25)**, then ascend **Upper Watergate Stairs (26A)** to the footpath leading to Watergate Street. If the tide is not right out, continue to the end of Borthwick Street, passing **Borthwick Wharf (25A)** and Paynes Wharf, and turn left into Watergate Street.

The wall here at Watergate Street belongs to **Convoys Wharf**, which occupies the site of the **Old Royal Naval Dockyard (27)**. At this point you can see over the wall the upper part of the **Master Shipwright's House (27B)** and the adjoining **Naval Offices**. Continue along Watergate Street and turn right into Prince Street. You quickly come to the entrance to Convoys Wharf, with the Convoys office just inside. Continue and turn right into Sayes Court Street, and then into **Sayes Court Park (28)**; bear left through the Park into Grove Street, then turn right. When you come to the **Princess of Wales (29)**, there is a view of the top of the **covered slipways (27C)** in the Old Dockyard. Further along Grove Street, you pass an old gateway **(27A)** into the Dockyard, now bricked up.

Continue for some distance along Grove Street until you come to two white arches on the right; this is the old **gateway (30A)** into the **Royal Victoria Victualling Yard**, the remaining buildings of which now form part of the **Pepys Estate (30)**. Go through the gateway, past the **Colonnade**, then bear left for **The Terrace (30B)**; continue ahead to the **Thames Path**, and turn right for the **Foreshore** buildings **(30C)**, and **Drake's Steps**. If you have time, go up-river along the Riverside Walk to **Deptford Wharf (31)**, **St Georges Stairs (32)**, and the **boundary stone**.

42 - DEPTFORD

Return through the Pepys Estate to Grove Street, turn left then right along Oxestalls Road. From the **bridge (34A)** there are views of the embankment covering the **Grand Surrey Canal (34)**; continue, noting on the right **Deptford Park School (35)**, and **Deptford Park (36)** ahead.

Turn left along Evelyn Street; you soon come to **Blackhorse Bridge (34B)**, which provides another view of the Surrey Canal route. Continue, noting on the right **Deptford Fire Station**, **St Lukes Church (37)** and **192 Evelyn Street**, until you come to Deptford High Street. Turn right for Deptford Station.

WALK no 3 (covering St Johns, the eastern part of Lewisham Way, Lewisham College, Stone House, St Johns Church). Distance approx 2 kilometres.

Try to make an advance arrangement - see the gazetteer- to view the interior of St Johns Church. Bear in mind that St Johns Station is closed on Saturdays and Sundays.

On leaving **St Johns Station (38)**, turn right over the bridge along St Johns Vale; you are now in the area known as **St Johns (39)**, turn left into **Albyn Road.** Walk along Albyn Road, noting in particular **nos 88/134 (39A)**, then turn right down **Admiral Street** into Brookmill Road. You are now almost opposite the entrance to **Deptford Pumping Station (40)**, with views of the old **Kent Waterworks head office and manager's House (40A)** and the **Cornish Engine House (40B)**. If you have time, turn right for **Brookmill Park (41)**, which provides a good view of the **Main Engine House (40C)** and return.

Turn left into **Friendly Street (42)**; after reaching **nos 12/26 (42A)**, retrace steps and turn left into Albyn Road. Turn left along **Lucas Street (43)**, and at the end turn left into **Lewisham Way (44)**.

Proceed along Lewisham Way until you reach St Johns Vale; there are many fine buildings on the way - see the gazetteer entries for Lewisham Way, and for **Stone House (46)** and **Lewisham College (45)**. Continue a short distance beyond St Johns Vale for **St Johns Church (47)**, try to see the interior, and the **Welsh Presbyterian Church (48)**, then retrace steps, turn right down St Johns Vale and you are soon back at St Johns Station

NEW CROSS

Gazetteer

Section 'A' NEW CROSS GATE
(See map on page 44)

1. New Cross Gate Station. The present station building on New Cross Road is basically c1844; the western section preserves its original appearance, the remainder is much altered.

> New Cross Station was opened on the London & Croydon Railway 1839; it was renamed New Cross Gate 1923. The line was run partly along the bed of the disused Croydon Canal. A large area of locomotive sheds and workshops to the west of the station operated from 1844 to 1947. The station was the northern terminus of the atmospheric railway 1846-7.
>
> The East London Railway to Wapping ran 1869-86 from an adjoining station, which was dismantled 1900; the line re-opened 1913 with a platform at New Cross Gate Station. The line is at present closed, but is due to re-open early 1998.
>
> The Croydon Canal ran from the Grand Surrey Canal at New Cross to Croydon via Brockley, Forest Hill and Sydenham, with 28 locks; it was opened 1809. *(See also Deptford 34.)* It closed in 1836 after purchase by the London & Croydon Railway. The canal route was in fact only partly used by the railway, it diverged considerably south of New Cross Gate; short canal sections survive at Anerley and (largely grassed) at Sydenham.
>
> The atmospheric railway was based on trains drawn along by air being sucked out of a large iron pipe laid between the rails. No locomotives were used, but the front carriage carried a piston on a bar which fitted the pipe. The air was sucked out by large steam engines in engine houses situated at New Cross, Forest Hill, South Norwood and Croydon. It was a very short-lived experiment.

The East London Line platform is the easternmost. Just to its south is a group of large stones, thought to be of canal origin.

The area of the New Cross locomotive Sheds and workshops is now taken up by the Sainsburys Superstore of 1996 and its vast car park.

Brighton Grove (1A) is a terrace of 1858 for workers at the locomotive sheds, of which it is the only reminder; recently and attractively restored, it is accessible by a footpath off Harts Lane.

2. New Cross Road (the A2) is a long road, over two kilometres in length, extending from the railway bridge of the South London Line (opened 1866) in the west, where it joins Old Kent Road, to Deptford Broadway in the east. There are two main road junctions - New Cross Gate, where it is joined by Queens Road; and the Marquis of Granby, where it is joined by Lewisham Way. The road passes two railway stations - New Cross Gate and New Cross - and has many fine terraces and groups of houses dating from the 1820s onwards.

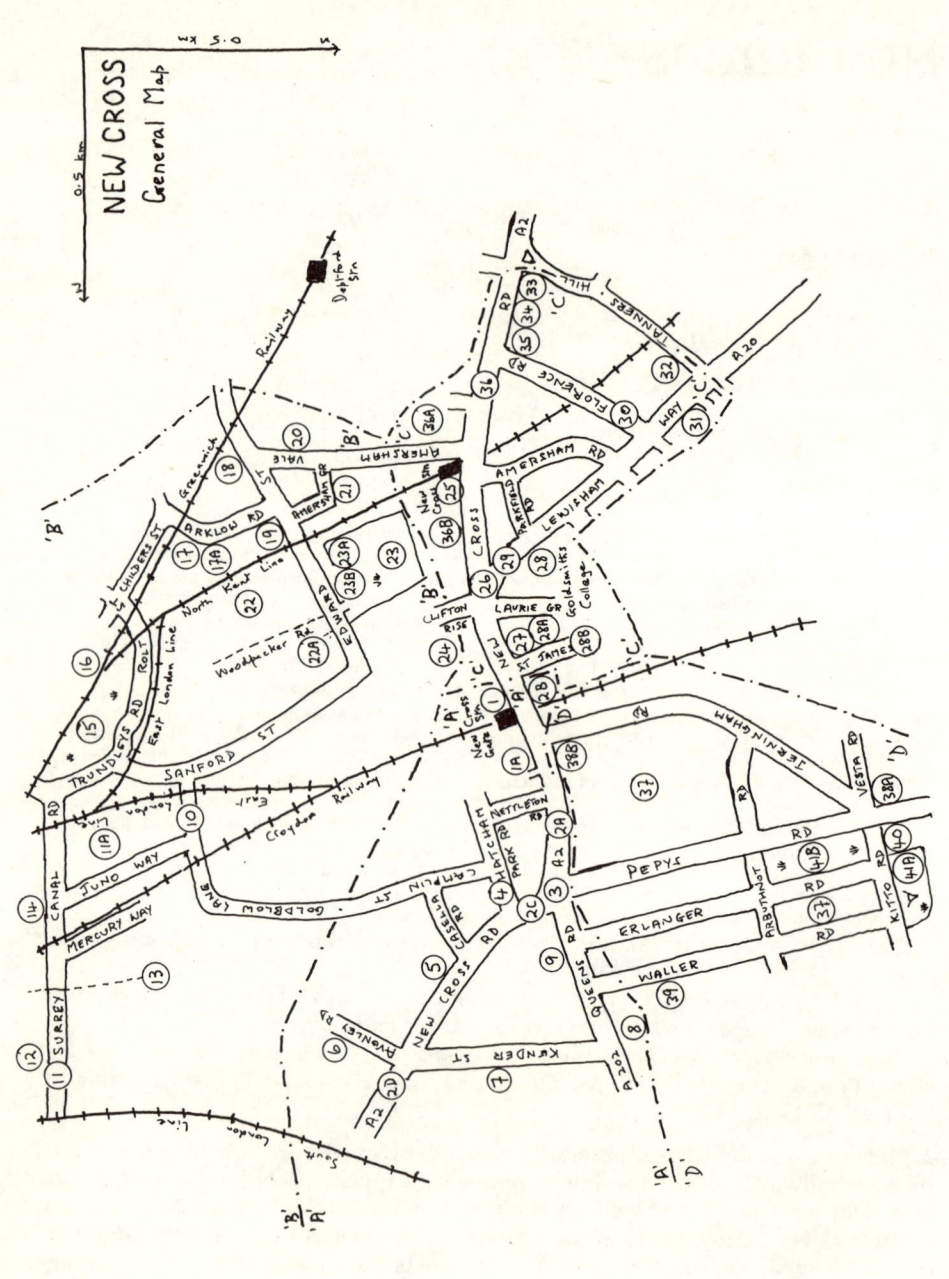

The western part only, from New Cross Gate Station to the South London Line railway bridge, is featured here. For the eastern part, continuing from New Cross Gate Station to Deptford Broadway, see 36.

Because of the abundance of buildings of interest, the gazetteer entries are split into three blocks, going from east to west. The even numbers are on the south side, the odd numbers on the north side.

New Cross Gate Station to New Cross Gate (2A):

The Rose Inn (2B), no 272, an attractive pub of 1855.

Nos 231/241, a terrace of tall Italianate houses, probably c1867 (though no 235 was skillfully rebuilt after the war). On no 241 is a Lewisham Council plaque: 'Sir Barnes Wallis, 1887-1979, pioneer of aircraft design, lived here 1892-1909'; he designed the Wellington bomber, and the bouncing bombs which destroyed the Mohne dam in the Ruhr Valley in 1943. On no 233 is a GLC blue plaque: 'John Tallis, 1816-1876, publisher of London Street Views, lived here'; the work was published 1838-40, and is of great value to London topographers. **Nos 243/255** are similar, c1868, as are houses in **Nettleton Road.** All these terraces were developed by the Haberdashers Company *(see also 37).*

Nos 223/229, c1842, a terrace with recessed pairs of entrances, linked to **no 221**, a large house c1842 with a fine porch.

*Nos 207/219, formerly known as **Hatcham Terrace**, a very fine tall terrace of 1841 with long rows of round-headed windows on the ground floor, and fine balcony railings.to the first floor.

Kingdom Hall, of Jehovahs Witnesses, no 210, a classical building of 1957, converted from the old South East London District Synagogue in the late 1980s. The first synagogue was established here in 1904.

New Cross Bus Depot, no 208, occupies the site of a London County Council tram depot, the largest in London, opened 1906, closed 1952; the buildings are now all modern.

For New Cross Gate, see 3.

New Cross Gate to Avonley Road / Kender Street (2C):

Clutch Clinic, no 182, was from 1909 to 1917 the **Electric Empire Cinema**.

Staffordshire Place, nos 170/178, of 1838, with modern shopfronts.

Five Bells, no 153, a fine classical pub of 1841 with quoins and deep eaves. Note the five bells between the eaves brackets. Later extension to the left.

Nos 109/117, nos 119/141 and **nos 143/147** are terraces c1870 above modern shopfronts. They were developed after the Haberdashers Company demolished Hatcham House, which was sited at the end of the present Casella Road, in 1869 *(see also 37)*. The mansion, originally medieval, rebuilt probably 1775, was the home of the Hardcastle family, merchants and philanthropists.

Nos 136/148, c1830, stuccoed above modern shopfronts.

Minerva Terrace, nos 120/128, a monumental unified composition of 1833 above protruding modern shopfronts, the end houses both having four giant pilasters.

New Cross Library, nos 116/118, a mildly baroque building of 1911, now a community music studio.

For All Saints Church, see 5.

Nos 92/110 form an interesting group. **The Hatcham Arms**, no 92, and no 94 are probably c1850. No 96, a small house, and no 98, which is taller, are probably c1840. Nos 100/102 are probably c1850. Nos 104/110 are two pairs, probably of the 1820s, nos 104/106 spoilt by the protruding modern shopfronts.

Nos 44/46, a nice stuccoed pair of 1827.

The Crown and Anchor, no 43, a pub of 1827, the ground floor altered.

Avonley Road / Kender Street to the railway bridge (2D):
Nos 32/34, a substantial attractive pair of 1827.

*****Nos 3/41** are the most interesting and varied group on New Cross Road; formerly known as **St James Place**, building started at the eastern end in 1827. Nos 3/5 are a small pair, of 1839. Nos 7/11, of 1842, are much taller and more impressive, forming a terrace with nos 13/15, of 1840. Nos 17/39 form a long terrace - nos 17/23 are of 1840; nos 25 (of 1835) and 27 (of 1830) have slim round columns; no 29, with fluted columns, is of 1830; nos 31/33, no 35 (with fluted columns) and nos 37/39 are all of 1828. St James Cottage, no 41, is an attractive detached house of 1827.

*****Carlton Cottages**, nos 6/8 and 10/12, highly attractive pairs of 1828; note the fine fluted pilasters with ammonite capitals (an ammonite is a fossilised shell - the motif was often used by the Brighton architect Amon Henry Wilds). There are other buildings with ammonite capitals further west, beyond the railway bridge.

3. New Cross Gate. On the road island at the junction, which was the site of a tollgate from 1813 to 1865, the toilet entrances have fine ironwork railings; and there is a ventilating pipe of 1897 which doubled as a lamppost - it is a fluted column by Macfarlanes Castings of Glasgow, with a most unusual vaguely Egyptian pattern based on a design by the famous Glasgow architect Alexander Thomson. This is not in as good condition as the one outside the New Cross Inn *(see 26)*, though it is likely to be restored in the near future.

Around the junction are: **197 New Cross Road**, a building c1910 with florid classical dressings, originally London & South Western Bank, now Barclays Bank.

397/401 Queens Road, a stuccoed house c1850 with fine bow windows extending through three storeys on either side of the doorway, though the ground floor bows have been cut into by horrible modern shopfronts. Adjoining is

The White Hart, 184 New Cross Road, an 1898 rebuild of a mid 19th century pub.

4. Hatcham Park Road. Nos 1/27 on the north side are c1850, and are partly stuccoed and rusticated. Along the south side are long Italianate terraces of 1864.

5. All Saints Church, New Cross Road, a bulky ragstone Gothic church of 1871, with a fine large rose window to the west. The interior *(phone 0171-639 3497)* is more imposing; note the apse shaped chancel with postwar stained glass, the rose window, the acutely pointed arcades, and a fine font inscribed 'to the memory of Alfred Hardcastle, born at Hatcham House 1791, died there 1842' *(see 2C)*.

Behind is **All Saints Institute & Sunday School**, a Gothic brick building of 1877, extended towards the church 1882.

6. New Cross Hospital, Avonley Road. Opened 1871, closed c1985. Only a few older buildings remain, including the physiotherapy department with its prominent turret, the doctors quarters, the matrons house, and part of the boundary wall. Part of the site remains in health authority use, now known as Wardalls Grove; the other part is now a housing estate.

7. 56 Kender Street. A substantial house, formerly known as Hatcham Lodge; the doorway is flanked by fluted columns, and there are fine round-headed windows with masks at the rear. It was originally of 1827, but was altered and enlarged in 1858 for George England.

> George England was one of the country's pioneer locomotive builders. He founded Hatcham Iron Works in 1840 in Pomeroy Street behind the house; the works expanded into locomotive production in the 1850s and 1860s, and over 250 locomotives were made here. It became Fairlie Engine & Steam Carriage Co from 1869, but closed in 1872. Nothing now remains of the works; part of the site became General Engine & Boiler Co from 1872 and later Reliance Foundry, and part was Enos Fruit Salt Works from 1878 to 1940.

Adjoining, **Georginia Terrace**, nos 24/54, is a fine group, probably c1827, with steps leading up to the first floor.

8. Somerville Estate, Queens Road. An intimate and attractive estate of 1978, with groups of dark red brick houses forming an intricate pattern of irregular clusters, mostly behind a large adventure playground on the main road.

Adjacent to the east is **New Cross Fire Station**, of 1894, an extraordinary extravaganza with steep conical roofs on rounded towers at either end, and a tall circular tower behind.

9. Hatcham Liberal Club, 369 Queens Road, a fantastic building c1911, with an oriel window above the porch, and decorated stonework. The club was established elsewhere in 1880, the date on the facade.

Adjacent is **371/373 Queens Road**, a fine pair c1840 with stuccoed ground floor and basement.

Further east is **387 Queens Road**, an odd small building of 1893 with decorated stonework.

NEW CROSS

Gazetteer

Section 'B' CANALS & RAILWAYS
(See map on page 44)

10. Coldblow Lane includes some extraordinary railway townscape, based on New Cross Gate Station and its dense network of sidings *(see 1)*. Start where Coldblow Lane turns sharply east, opposite the old Den site of Millwall Football Club, now a housing estate. Going eastwards to Sanford Street:
   old railway track on the road, the site of Cold Blow Crossing, a level crossing on the Deptford Wharf branch, closed 1963 *(see Deptford 31)*;
   the bridge piers of an old siding into the Signal Works;
   a very narrow road tunnel, a brick arch c1854 of the Croydon Railway, widened by iron extensions with wider arches on either side which take additional tracks;
   Juno Way, with the Mazawattee tower visible *(see 11A)*;
   a long tunnel under Millwall Football Club car park, which was formerly Coldblow Farm and some railway sidings;
   finally, the road goes under a modern iron bridge of the East London Line to Wapping.

11. Surrey Canal Road, constructed c1980, follows the bed of the Grand Surrey Canal *(see also Deptford 34)*. The towpath, paved in part, and the canal edge are still there on the north side. Going from west to east, from Ilderton Road:
   a modern iron bridge of the South London Line to Queens Road Peckham;
   a timber shed with a prominent canopy of Harcros, the only survivor of many timber yards on the canal route;
   the footbridge to Bridge House Meadows, *see 13*;
   on the right, the beginning of Mercury Way, on the site of the former junction of the Surrey and Croydon Canals;
   a brick arch of the Croydon Railway to New Cross Gate;
   on the right, the **Elizabeth Industrial Estate (11A)**, on the site of the Mazawattee Tea Company works, which here produced chocolate and cocoa from 1901 to c1955 - the main large tower has gone, but the angled corner at the front, as well as the smaller tower at the rear and some buildings nearby have survived;
   on the left, Landmann Way and SELCHP, *see 14*;
   a modern iron bridge of the East London Railway, carrying lines from both New Cross and New Cross Gate Stations;
   bearing left, a brick arch carrying both the North Kent Line to New Cross and the Greenwich Railway to Deptford.

12. The Den, the grounds of Millwall Football Club, a fantastic high-tech structure consisting of four great stands. It opened 1993 when the Club moved from its old grounds at Coldblow Lane, south of Bridge House Meadows *(see below)*. Access is via Zampa Road. Alongside is Lewisham Lions Leisure Centre, also high-tech 1993.

> Millwall FC was founded as Millwall Rovers FC in 1885 by workers at Mortons jam & marmalade factory at Westferry Road, Isle of Dogs. They used several grounds in the southern part of the Isle of Dogs, but they were found difficult of access, and they moved to Coldblow Lane, New Cross, in 1910. They changed their name to Millwall Athletic FC in 1889, and to Millwall FC in 1899. It was in 1899 that they first began to be commonly called The Lions.

13. Bridge House Meadows is an extensive area of open space, opened 1981 on the site of New Cross Stadium (opened 1913, closed 1969). A hilly mound gives a fine view all around. The old Den site of Millwall Football Club, now a housing estate, was to the south.

To the north a footpath leads across a modern footbridge over Surrey Canal Road; the footbridge replaced a railway bridge (note the brick base below) which carried an early branch of the East London Line from Peckham. This branch may be reinstated if a proposed extension of the East London Line to East Dulwich goes ahead.

The footpath leads between The Den and SELCHP under three railway arches, and is another remarkable example of railway townscape - first, a modern bridge of the Croydon railway; then a brick bridge of the North Kent Line; and then a wider brick bridge carrying both the Bricklayers Arms branch of 1844 and the Greenwich Railway. (NB. At this point the Greenwich Railway and the North Kent Line diverge to form two road arches, even though they have already joined further east at North Kent East Junction, *see 16*.) However, the footpath may in the future be taken up by the proposed extension to the East London Line.

14. SELCHP (South East London Combined Heat and Power Ltd), off Landmann Way, a road which was built on the line of the Deptford Wharf siding which closed 1963 *(see Deptford 31)*. A large waste-to-energy incinerator of 1994, the first such high-technology plant in Britain; it deals with the refuse of the London Boroughs of Greenwich and Lewisham, as well as other boroughs and private companies.

Looking at the great silver building from the south, with its 100 metre tall round chimney to the right, the largest part of the structure is the boiler house, with its blue tube framework; the storage pit is to the left, and further left at the end are the turbine hall and condensers.

The site lies between, to the north, the combined lines of the Greenwich Railway to Deptford and the North Kent Line to New Cross, and to the west, the Croydon Railway to New Cross Gate.

15. Folkestone Gardens, an open space laid out after the war, well landscaped with a lake and island; seven large housing blocks built by the South Eastern Railway in 1914 had been on the site, and were badly damaged during the war.

16. North Kent East Junction, Rolt Street. This is where the viaducts of the London & Greenwich Railway (of 1836) and the North Kent Line (of 1849) meet. Note the skewed arches, with nice brickwork, under both lines (there is a similar skewed arch further east at Edward Street, Deptford). Further west in Rolt Street the East London Line (of 1869) emerges at street level, opposite Folkestone Gardens.

17. Former Stones Works. The industrial estate with its entrance in Arklow Road was from 1881 to 1969 the site of the Stones engineering works.

> J. Stone & Co was founded by Josiah Stone in a small workshop by St Nicholas Church Deptford 1831, making copper nails, rivets etc. In 1842 it moved to the arches by Deptford Station, where in due course they made handpumps and manual fire engines. The company moved to Arklow Road 1881, making propellers, watertight ships doors, steam pumps, electric lighting systems for railways, other railway equipment, and a variety of other engineering products, though propellers came to be the main product. The propeller foundry moved to Charlton 1916. By 1950 the Deptford plant was responsible for rail and road transport products, nails, rivets and washers. In 1959 the firm became Stone Platt Industries, and in 1963 Stone Manganese Marine. The move to Crawley (later to Harlow) began in 1966, and the Deptford factory closed 1969.

A range of old Stones workshops, of 1903-07, survives along Childers Street. Further along Arklow Road is the **former Stones Office Building (17A)**, a handsome classical building of 1916, with an extra floor added 1928.

18. Celestial Church of Christ, Edward Street, an extraordinary Gothic building of 1883, originally St Marks Church.

19. Olivet Deptford Baptist Church, Arklow Road, a striking church of 1980, with steeply sloping roof and elongated squared windows.

20. Deptford Police Station, Amersham Vale, a handsome building of 1912 in Queen Anne style, with gently bowed windows through two floors, and distinctive wrought iron railings.

21. 38 Amersham Grove, a red brick Italianate house, probably c1865, which has lost its former porch, but retains massive stone balls on the forecourt walls. The derelict building next door was formerly a private museum of curios collected by a merchant navy captain, established 1890. The terraces in Amersham Grove were also built in the 1860s.

22. Milton Court Estate. This estate of the late 1960s is in the course of improvement, with its tower blocks being either demolished or refurbished. **Woodpecker Road**, now pedestrianised, follows the route of an old lane as it curves through the estate. **Ludwick Mews (22A)** is a very attractive close, with steep roofs of black slate, of 1979.

23. Fordham Park, a large cleared area of the 1970s; the landmarks around it are the **Moonshot Community Centre (23A)**, a red brick building of 1981 (note on the rear wall the large and striking multi-coloured brickwork pattern forming a human face), and **Dew Drop Inn (23B)**, a pub of the 1860s.

24. Childeric School. The smaller building by the entrance is of 1892, the larger building, impressive and towering starkly over the surrounding area, of 1899.

NEW CROSS

Gazetteer

Section 'C' NEW CROSS
(See map on page 44)

25. New Cross Station was opened as New Cross & Naval School Station *(see 28)* on the North Kent Line in 1850; it was renamed New Cross 1854. The platform for the East London Railway to Wapping, on the eastern side, opened 1884. The old station building was demolished 1975 and replaced by temporary buildings, and the bridge rebuilt. The present modern building in Amersham Vale is of 1985. The down platform retains some ornate iron columns of the original station.

26. The Marquis of Granby. This road junction takes its name from the pub **Marquis of Granby**, 322 New Cross Road; there has been a pub here since c1760, though the present building is of 1868. This was the original village centre of New Cross, which is said to have taken its name from an old pub, New Cross House, 316 New Cross Road, now known as the **Goldsmiths Tavern**, the present building being of 1895.

Opposite is **New Cross Inn**, 323 New Cross Road, a riotously fanciful pub c1890 (note the line of winged caryatids along both sides), on the site of an early 18th century pub. The original New Cross tollgate was located here, at the top of Clifton Rise, from 1718 to 1813. Outside the pub is a lamppost of 1897 which doubled as a ventilating pipe to former public toilets, a fluted column by Macfarlanes Castings of Glasgow, with a most unusual vaguely Egyptian pattern based on a design by the famous Glasgow architect Alexander Thomson *(see also 3)*; it was originally on the road island.

The **former Gaumont Cinema** (opened as New Cross Kinema 1925, closed 1960) is now painted black, and houses a furniture store and a night-club. Adjacent is **337 New Cross Road**, formerly Midland Bank, now disused; it is of 1905, with four great Tuscan columns between classical entrances at either end. **Nos 339/345** adjoining are basically of 1827 but the modern shopfronts make this difficult to appreciate.

27. *Deptford Town Hall, built 1905 by Lanchester & Rickards, has an extraordinarily elaborate stone facade decorated with architectural sculpture. The doorway is headed by two figures of dolphin-tailed Tritons swirling out as corbels to support a large oriel decorated with a ship's prow and other marine carvings. Along the first floor are four statues of admirals - Drake with the date 1587, Blake date 1652, Nelson date 1805, and a 'conventional representation of an admiral in 1905 which does not represent any particular admiral'. The pediment contains a sculpture of an old naval battle, and is topped by a short clock tower with a galleon weathervane (a replica of 1994). The end bays are recessed, one with paired columns (like other ground floor windows), the other with the Deptford coat of arms and a crab over the archway. The building is in use by Deptford City Challenge until 1997, when it is likely to become part of Goldsmiths College.

The ***interior** too has lavish decoration. The vestibule opens out into a marble-paved entrance hall with four great marble columns, lit by a dome in an elaborately plastered ceiling; a grand marble staircase with magnificent ornate wrought iron railings branches into two arms which lead up to a gallery with paired marble Ionic columns. The gallery leads back to the doorway of the old council chamber, surrounded by extravagant plasterwork. The council chamber has elaborate plasterwork, and a projecting oval balcony corresponding to the external oriel.

Adjacent is **288 New Cross Road**, formerly called Hope Cottage, a brick building of 1842, with a prominent porch supported by solid pillars. It is in use by Goldsmiths College.

28. *Goldsmiths College. The frontage and the long side ranges of the main building, on Lewisham Way, were built in Renaissance style by John Shaw in 1844 as the Royal Naval School. The building is dignified, of red brick with stone dressings, with a classical doorcase, the top of which lines up with a guilloche course which continues right round the original building. Above the doorcase is the Goldsmiths coat of arms. The roofline was changed, losing its pitched roof and many finials, after war damage.

> The Royal Naval School was intended for the sons of 'less affluent naval and marine officers'. It moved to Fairy Hall in Mottingham in 1889, staying until 1911 in a building which then became Eltham College.
>
> This building re-opened as the Goldsmiths Company's Technical & Recreative Institute in 1891, and formally became part of London University as Goldsmiths College in 1905. It was mainly a Teachers Training College, the largest in Britain at the time, and a School of Art. It now has 4500 full-time students, and specialises in visual & performing arts, media & communications, as well as humanities, education, social sciences, mathematics. The college's special relationship with the local community is unique in London University; it offers part-time as well as full-time courses, and evening courses for adults leading to degrees.

The entrance hall (note the Royal Naval School plaque) leads directly into the Great Hall, of 1891, which is roofed over the former school's parade ground. The open square at the rear was closed by a block of 1907 designed by Sir Reginald Blomfield; the garden front of this building is baroque and monumental, with four great pilasters and circular windows. To the left of the garden front, the old chapel, probably by John Shaw 1851, has Venetian windows and circular windows, but is difficult to see because of later buildings; it was converted to become the George Wood Theatre 1964.

The main building is now the centre of an amazing complex of buildings.

Going westwards along Lewisham Way, linked to the main building are: the **Students Union** of 1975, bridging Dixon Road; the **Education Building** of 1968; **Warmington Tower**, an obtrusively high hall of residence of 1969; and the **Information Services Building** of 1997. All are in white modernist style, though note the **Goldsmiths Gallery** of 1975, a brick octagon, no longer used as a gallery. The Information Services Building is linked to the **Library**, a vernacular brick building, slightly high-tech, of 1988.

Around the large recreation space at the rear are **Whitehead Building**, to the right, of 1968, and **Lockwood Building**, of 1962, both modernist, with lots of outbuildings. Note, in front of the tennis courts, an old Kent / Surrey boundary marker.

In Laurie Grove is the **Laurie Grove Baths (28A)** designed by Thomas Dinwiddy 1898, closed 1991, now the Research & Development Precinct of Goldsmiths. This red brick and stone building is of an intricate and dense design, in a sort of Jacobean style, and has a bold archway to the left. The houses in Laurie Grove, of the 1860s, now form part of Goldsmiths.

Laurie Grove leads to the **Laban Centre for Movement and Dance**, which occupies a warren of corridors and studios embracing the former **St James Church (28B)**, a Gothic ragstone building of 1854, as well as the adjoining church school of 1865. The exterior of the old church can be viewed closing the end of the road called St James. The buildings were converted 1973-89; archways, stained glass, and other church furnishings now form a bizarre backcloth to the interior of the Laban Centre. The Bonnie Bird Theatre in the Centre was opened 1989.

> The Laban Centre has links with Goldsmiths, but its courses are mostly validated by the City University, London. It was founded 1945 by Rudolf Laban (1879-1958), the pioneer and founder of European Modern Dance.

The modern St James Church of 1982, a small basic brick building converted from a youth club building of c1962, is to the right at the end of St James.

Some houses with fancifully decorated doorcases, probably of the 1870s, remain at the end of St James, and now form part of Goldsmiths. The long block opposite is a Goldsmiths hall of residence of 1997.

29. Lewisham Way. *The western part, from the Marquis of Granby to Upper Brockley Road / Tanners Hill, is featured here. For the eastern part, continuing to Loampit Hill, see Deptford 44. The even numbers are on the south side, the odd numbers on the north side. Going from west to east:*

Nos 9/31 are the terraced shops opposite Goldsmiths; the modern ground floors spoil the pleasing effect of the upper floors, which are of the early 1850s.

Nos 41/53, an attractive Italianate terrace of 1854, in part used by Goldsmiths.

Parkfield Road, laid out c1850, has three pairs with strong porches to the south and a short Italianate terrace to the north.

Nos 55/71, a gabled Italianate group, mostly pairs, built 1846-52.

Gloucester Terrace, nos 32/42, a pleasant Italianate terrace, used by Goldsmiths, is inscribed 1860 but was actually built 1855.

The Rosemary Branch, no 44, an attractive pub of 1854.

Nos 60/68 is a terrace of houses with strong Ionic porches, of 1857-60.

Nos 70/72 and **74/76**, of 1857, have recessed porches with Doric columns.

Amersham Road has long terraces on both sides of the early 1850s.

Surrey House, no 80, a substantial and attractive house of 1860 with an ornamental doorcase round the corner in Shardeloes Road, now in use by Goldsmiths College. The adjoining groups **nos 82/110** are Italianate, 1857-61.

Nos 119/133, formerly called Cambridge Terrace, particularly elegant, of 1848.

54 - NEW CROSS

For Florence Road, see 30. For Deptford Library, see 31.

Flower of Kent, no 135, a pleasant pub of 1846. Adjoining, **Albert Place**, nos 137/143, a pleasing terrace of 1864; and **Alexandra Place**, nos 145/7, a pair of 1863.

Nos 165/169, a white tiled building of 1935, was formerly part of Pynes department store, and features the letter P in many places.

30. Florence Road retains several long terraces of Italianate houses c1847, many with carved wreaths on the doorcases, some with pilaster strips.

31. *Deptford Library, a grand baroque building of 1914 by Sir Alfred Brumwell Thomas, now used as an art gallery, with artists' studios and workshops. The frontage has six monumental Ionic columns flanked by two Ionic pilasters.

The **interior** is impressive - note the long rows of round-headed windows along the ground floor, and the grand staircase lit by a Venetian window, leading up to a gallery with a fine barrel-vaulted glass roof.

32. Kylefield House, 124 Tanners Hill. This is a mansion of 1789, originally called **Brunswick House**; its grounds extended up to Lewisham Way. Only small sections of the house are now visible: in Tanners Hill - on the south face, the end bay with a Coade stone medallion of a woman and child; and from Alexandra Cottages (an industrial estate in Lewisham Way), a full-height bay to the west. The remainder of the building was obscured from 1850 by 126 Tanners Hill being built hard against it.

33. Addey & Stanhope School, New Cross Road. A dignified red brick building of 1899 by Sir Alfred Brumwell Thomas. It is L-shaped, with prominent gables and a grand doorcase. Note the fine plane trees in the front courtyard.

> The establishment of the school was the outcome of the amalgamation in 1899 of two older Deptford charity schools. Addey School, built 1821 in Church Street, resulted from a bequest of land by John Addey, master shipwright at the Naval Dockyard, who died 1606. Dean Stanhopes School, built 1723 in High Street, resulted from a charity set up by George Stanhope, who died 1727; he had been vicar of both St Nicholas Deptford and St Marys Lewisham, as well as Dean of Canterbury. A tablet to Addey is on the north wall of St Nicholas Church *(see Deptford 23)*; and a tablet to Stanhope is in St Marys Church *(see Lewisham 63)*.

A statue of a charity girl which was one of a pair on the front of the Stanhope school of 1723 is now in the entrance hall of the School, as is a tablet of 1906 to commemorate the tercentenary of the death of John Addey.

34. Iyengar Yoga Institute, 470 New Cross Road. This striking white building with its classical facade is a rebuild by the New Cross Building Society during the interwar period. The inscription on the facade 'established 1866' refers to the Building Society, which was founded in an already existing building on this site in 1866, and moved away 1975. It was used by Millwall Football Club from 1980, the Seventh Day Adventist Mission from 1986, and the yoga institute from 1994.

> The New Cross Building Society was founded here in 1866. In 1975 it moved its head office to 58 Deptford High Street. It ceased trading in 1983, and transferred its engagements to the Woolwich Building Society in 1984.

35. *Zion Baptist Chapel, New Cross Road. The almost monumental facade of this handsome classical brick building is of 1876. It has great round-headed doorcase and windows, four giant pilasters, and a fine pediment with a circular window. It is set back within a courtyard cut off from the street by railings with a fine lamp-holder; on either side are **466 & 468 New Cross Road**, similar classical houses c1850.

> ,A chapel was originally opened on this site in 1846. A new chapel was added in front 1857, and the original chapel became the Sunday School building; it is now used as the church hall, the original pulpit being in a room upstairs. The chapel was extended with a new facade 1876. The Sunday School building was extended 1864 and 1886.

The ***interior** is magnificent, with a gallery all round fronted by finely carved decorative iron railings.

> *As the original building is at the rear, it cannot be seen without access to the courtyard. Those with a special interest in viewing the original building and the interior of the chapel should contact the minister on 0181-691 6586 to make an appointment.*

36. New Cross Road. *See also 2. The eastern part, from Deptford Broadway to the Marquis of Granby, is featured here. For the western part, from Old Kent Road to New Cross Gate Station, see 2. For Addey & Stanhope School, see 33. For the old New Cross Building Society, see 34. For Zion Chapel, see 35. The even numbers are on the south side, the odd numbers on the north side. Going from east to west:*

Royal Albert, no 460, now called Paradise Bar, is an interesting pub c1850; the front entrance has a Tudor archway and is framed by bulbous granite pilasters, and there are elegantly curved bow windows to the front and the side.

Nos 459/481 are basically early 19th century or in some cases late 18th century, though much altered and with modern ground floors. No 469 has an early 19th century bow at first floor level.

No 455 is the old office of Clark Bunnett & Co, 1880, with a narrow recessed entrance framed by Corinthian columns. The works were behind in Glenville Grove, making steam engines, roller shutters and cranes 1820-1914, but no trace remains. Note the fragment of an old iron gas lamp to the east of the entrance.

Florence Terrace, nos 416/458, a long Italianate terrace c1850. Some remain as houses, with stuccoed and rusticated ground floors, others are converted to shops.

Mornington Centre (36A), Stanley Street. A harmonious London School Board building of 1879, with a dominant skyline.

Nos 409/443, a long Italianate group, a pair and two terraces, c1850.

For New Cross Station, see 25.

The Walpole (36B), no 407, a pub basically c1855, but much altered; it has fine Victorian tiling inside and old cast iron gas lamps in front.

High up outside the adjoining no 405 is a **tobacco roll**, a rare survival of a Victorian trade sign, probably of the 1870s; the shop ceased to be a tobacconist c1994, and is now a post office.

Harvey Terrace, nos 338/350, a fine Italianate unified group with anthemion motifs to the first floor windows, the ground floors stuccoed and rusticated. It bears the incised date 1834; this is incorrect, it is of 1851.

For the Marquis of Granby, see 26. For Deptford Town Hall, see 27.

NEW CROSS

Gazetteer

Section 'D' TELEGRAPH HILL
(See map on page 44)

37. Hatcham Manor Estate, also known as the New Cross Estate, was built by the Haberdashers Company to a layout by their surveyor William Snooke between 1875 and 1900. The first road to be developed was **Pepys Road**, with a pattern of houses in Gothic style to the north and Edwardian style to the south. **Jerningham Road** was developed with a similar pattern from the 1880s. The other north-south roads, **Erlanger Road** and **Waller Road**, were developed from the 1880s in predominantly Edwardian style. Because of the length of the principal roads and the lack of variety in house design, the overall effect can seem rather monotonous.

> The Haberdashers Company is one of the 12 great livery companies of the City of London, which were originally medieval trade guilds; it is known to have existed in 1371, and it reached its zenith of power and influence in the Tudor period. Its function began to change to administering charities in the late 17th century.
>
> In 1614 the Company acquired the manor of Hatcham. In c1867-68 they built some large houses on the north side of New Cross Road *(see 2A)*. In 1869, after the Hardcastle family had ceased to live there, they demolished the manor house, Hatcham House *(see 2C)*, and developed the grounds. The Hatcham Manor Estate leading up to Telegraph Hill was their largest housing development. The Haberdashers property mark can be seen on many corner buildings throughout the area.

38. Haberdashers Askes Hatcham College. The college is in two parts - the **Boys School (38A)**, built 1875 on a hilly site at the top of Pepys Road, and the **Girls School (38B)**, built 1891 at the bottom of Jerningham Road.

> The two schools came together as Hatcham College in 1991. The principal sponsor is the Robert Aske Foundation, one of many charities administered by the Haberdashers Company. Robert Aske, a haberdasher, died 1689, leaving in his will money to establish almshouses and a boys school, which was originally at Hoxton. The schools at New Cross were erected out of the same endowment in 1875, and the Hoxton school was sold in 1898. Other Haberdashers Schools within the Aske Foundation are at Elstree.

The first stage, designed by William Snooke 1875, consisted of two large and similar blocks on a magnificent site at the top of the hill with the ground sloping away steeply all around; the Boys School occupied the block facing Pepys Road and the Girls School the block facing Vesta Road. Both blocks were in yellow stock brick, Gothic style, with strange steeply gabled towers over the entrance. After the new Girls School *(see below)* was built in 1891, both blocks were used for the Boys School. In 1907 a handsome low pavilion-like building (containing the Main Hall) was added between the two blocks. The complex includes many later buildings, including the gymnasium and art room of 1936, at right angles to the Vesta Road building, and many postwar extensions.

On the green in front of the central block is a statue of 1836 of Robert Aske. It is a copy made of Coade stone of an earlier statue of Aske, in Haberdashers robes, leaning on a plinth and holding building plans in his hand; the statue with its original inscriptions was moved here from Hoxton 1903.

Note also two short cast iron posts alongside each other on Vesta Road at the eastern end of the site - one is a Haberdashers property mark, the other an old Kent / Surrey boundary marker.

The Girls School, by Henry Stock 1891, is a large and attractive multi-gabled red brick building in Queen Anne style, with a splendid Tudor doorcase and fantastic gargoyles. In front is the Connaught Wing of 1936, and many postwar extensions.

39. Edmund Waller School, Waller Road, has a handsome London School Board building of 1887 in Queen Anne style, and a less appealing second building of 1899 to the south.

40. Church of St Catherine, Pepys Road, built 1893 by Henry Stock for the Haberdashers Company, is a bulky ragstone church with elongated Gothic windows. The north transept is castellated; the south transept has a separate roof. The chancel was extended in 1913.

The west end was incorporated into Telegraph Hill Neighbourhood Centre in 1970; a nicely designed screen in the Centre gives a good view of the church interior, which is of red brick and imposing - *for a better view contact the vicarage next door, or telephone 0181-639 1050.*

The vicarage next door is contemporary with the church, and is of interest as the only red brick house in a predominantly stock brick area.

41. Telegraph Hill Park, opened 1895, is in two parts. The southern section **(41A)**, off Kitto Road, provides, from its highest point (at 45 metres) in the grassed centre, fantastic panoramic *views over Central and West London. The northern section **(41B)**, between Pepys Road and Erlanger Road, is larger but of less interest.

> An Admiralty semaphore telegraph station was erected here in 1796, and remained in use until 1823.

NEW CROSS

Suggested Walks

It is recommended that the suggested walks be followed in conjunction with the Gazetteer and the map, and that the Gazetteer be consulted at each location for a detailed description.

Walk no 1 covers Section 'A', and Walk no 2 Section 'C'. Most locations in these two sections are covered; some other locations have not been included, as they might add too much to the length of the walks. The walks follow a more or less circular route, so they can be joined at any location. Walk no 1 begins and ends at New Cross Gate Station, and Walk no 2 at the Marquis of Granby, just west of New Cross Station.

Section 'B' is not included, as the gazetteer already includes two suggested routes; the other locations follow a logical sequence within a compact area, and there is no need to suggest a particular route. Section 'D' is not included, as the locations are thinly spread over quite a large area..

WALK no 1 (including New Cross Gate and the western part of New Cross Road). Distance approx 2 kilometres.

(NB. It is worth trying to make an advance arrangement - see the Gazetteer - to view the interior of All Saints Church.)

On leaving **New Cross Gate Station (1)**, note **The Rose Inn (2B)** opposite, turn right into Harts Lane to see **Brighton Grove (1A)**, and return to New Cross Road. The best way to see **New Cross Road (2)** is to proceed block by block, as in the gazetteer, noting the buildings on both sides.

First the block from New Cross Gate Station westwards to the road junction of New Cross Gate **(2A)**. At **New Cross Gate (3)** note the ventilating pipe and toilet railings on the road island, and the buildings all around. Continue to the block westwards to Avonley Road / Kender Street **(2C)**. On the way proceed a short distance down **Hatcham Park Road (4)**, and note **All Saints Church (5)**, try to see the interior. Then continue to the block westwards to the railway bridge **(2D)**.

Retrace steps a short way, then turn right along **Kender Street** and continue to the end, passing **Georginia Terrace** and **no 56 (7)**. Turn left into Queens Road, noting the **Somerville Estate** and **New Cross Fire Station (8)** on the right side, and **Hatcham Liberal Club (9)** and other buildings on the left side. On reaching the New Cross Gate road junction, continue straight ahead until you are back at New Cross Gate Station.

WALK no 2 (including the Marquis of Granby, Deptford Town Hall, Goldsmiths College, the western part of Lewisham Way, and the eastern part of New Cross Road). Distance approx 3 kilometres.

(NB. It is worth trying to make an advance arrangement - see the Gazetteer - to view the interior of Zion Baptist Chapel.)

At the road junction called **The Marquis of Granby (26)**, note the buildings all around - **New Cross Inn** (and the ventilating pipe), **Deptford Town Hall (27)** and **no 288**, the **Goldsmiths Tavern**, and the pub **Marquis of Granby**. Go up **Laurie Grove** to see the **Baths (28A)**, then from the junction bear right past the buildings of **Goldsmiths College (28)**. If you have time, go through the main building to see the garden front and the buildings behind.

Continue along **Lewisham Way (29)**, noting the buildings on both sides. Proceed a short way down **Florence Road (30)**, then retrace steps. Note **Deptford Library (31)** as you continue along Lewisham Way. When you reach Tanners Hill, turn left, noting **Kylefield House (32)**.

At the bottom of Tanners Hill, turn left and you immediately come to **Addey & Stanhope School (33)** and **Iyengar Yoga Institute (34)**; then you come to **Zion Chapel (35)** - try to see the interior. Continue along **New Cross Road (36)**, noting buildings on both sides and passing **New Cross Station (25)**, until you are back at the Marquis of Granby.

BROCKLEY

Introduction

The manor of Brockley was in existence at least by the 12th century. A Premonstratensian Abbey was founded here c1187, the site probably being near the present St Peters Church, Wickham Road; but it moved to Bayham Abbey (near Tunbridge Wells) soon afterwards in 1200.

Brockley now forms an oblong less than a kilometre wide, but stretching over two kilometres from Lewisham Way in the north to Forest Hill in the south. The northern part, known as Upper Brockley, which was in the old parish of Deptford, contains a great concentration of Victorian housing dating from the 1850s to the 1880s; the southern part, around Crofton Park, which was in the old parish of Lewisham, developed mainly from the 1890s around minor shopping centres in Brockley Road.

The lane from Deptford to Sydenham

In 1800 Brockley was a rural settlement on an old lane which ran from Deptford to Sydenham. The lane started as Butt Lane (which subsequently became Deptford High Street and Tanners Hill), then entered Brockley along the line of Upper Brockley Road and ran to Deptford Common, which was situated near the present Brockley Cross. It then continued via the present Coulgate Street and Brockley Road to Brockley Green; this was quite a picturesque spot, with the Brockley Jack inn, predecessor of the present pub, and Brockley Hall, an early 18th century mansion (it was demolished in 1932 and Brockley Hall Road is now on the site). From Brockley Green the lane continued to Forest Hill and Sydenham, and another lane went eastwards to Ladywell and Lewisham.

Upper Brockley

The residential area of Upper Brockley was largely developed as two great estates - the Wickham Park Estate and the Tyrwhitt-Drake Estate.

A relatively small area in the west consists mainly of standard terraces of the 1850s. Further east is the most dramatic part of Brockley - four long wide roads with large houses - Wickham Road, the widest, with the largest houses, and Breakspears Road, in the Wickham Park Estate; then Tressillian Road and Tyrwhitt Road, in the Tyrwhitt-Drake Estate.

These roads were laid out by 1851, when the first two houses in Wickham Road were built; but development proceeded slowly, with only seven houses in Wickham Road completed by 1859, when the first houses in Tyrwhitt Road were built. Both roads had developed some way southwards by 1868, when the first houses in Breakspears Road and Tressillian Road were built. From that time development continued steadily, and by 1885 was virtually complete.

Up to the mid 1860s the houses were predominantly in an Italianate style, but from this point Gothic influences began to emerge and during the 1870s became dominant. The Gothic influence manifests itself mainly in wide gables and also in the doorcases, which often have strange capitals. Many houses have other fanciful decorative features, and in some cases the ornamentation is so extravagant that it has to be seen to be believed. But it is odd that the pointed arch, probably the most potent symbol of Gothic architecture, occurs in relatively few Brockley houses.

There are also groups of interesting houses in many of the shorter roads running horizontally across the estate; and in Upper Brockley Road there is a sort of urban village, with a fine shopping parade and two pubs, all of the 1860s.

South of Tyrwhitt Road and Tressillian Road is the great mound of Hilly Fields, with its spectacular views and Prendergast School perched on the top.

Brockley Cross and Crofton Park

The Croydon Railway was opened in 1839, in part using the bed of the disused Croydon Canal; from New Cross Gate Station southwards, once past the Goldsmiths College complex, it largely defines the western boundary of Brockley.

Brockley Cross is now a complicated but important road junction, near the rail junction of the Croydon Line and the Nunhead Loop Line. Brockley Station on the Croydon Line opened in 1871; and Brockley Lane Station on the Greenwich Park Line in 1872. (Brockley Lane Station closed when the Greenwich Park Line closed in 1917; part of the line was brought back into use from 1929 as the Nunhead Loop Line.)

Before the railway stations opened, in the 1860s, the Breakspeare Arms had appeared in Brockley Road, and groups of Italianate houses in Cranfield Road and Foxberry Road. Further south in Brockley Road was Brockley Cemetery, which opened as Deptford Cemetery in 1858 and merged with Lewisham (now Ladywell) Cemetery to the east in 1965.

Otherwise, the area around Brockley Road developed from the 1880s, and gathered momentum from the 1890s. In 1892 Crofton Park Station, on the Catford Loop Line, was opened at the northern edge of the site of the old Brockley Green; this was followed by a minor shopping centre which became known as Crofton Park and the development of the roads off Brockley Road to the south towards Forest Hill.

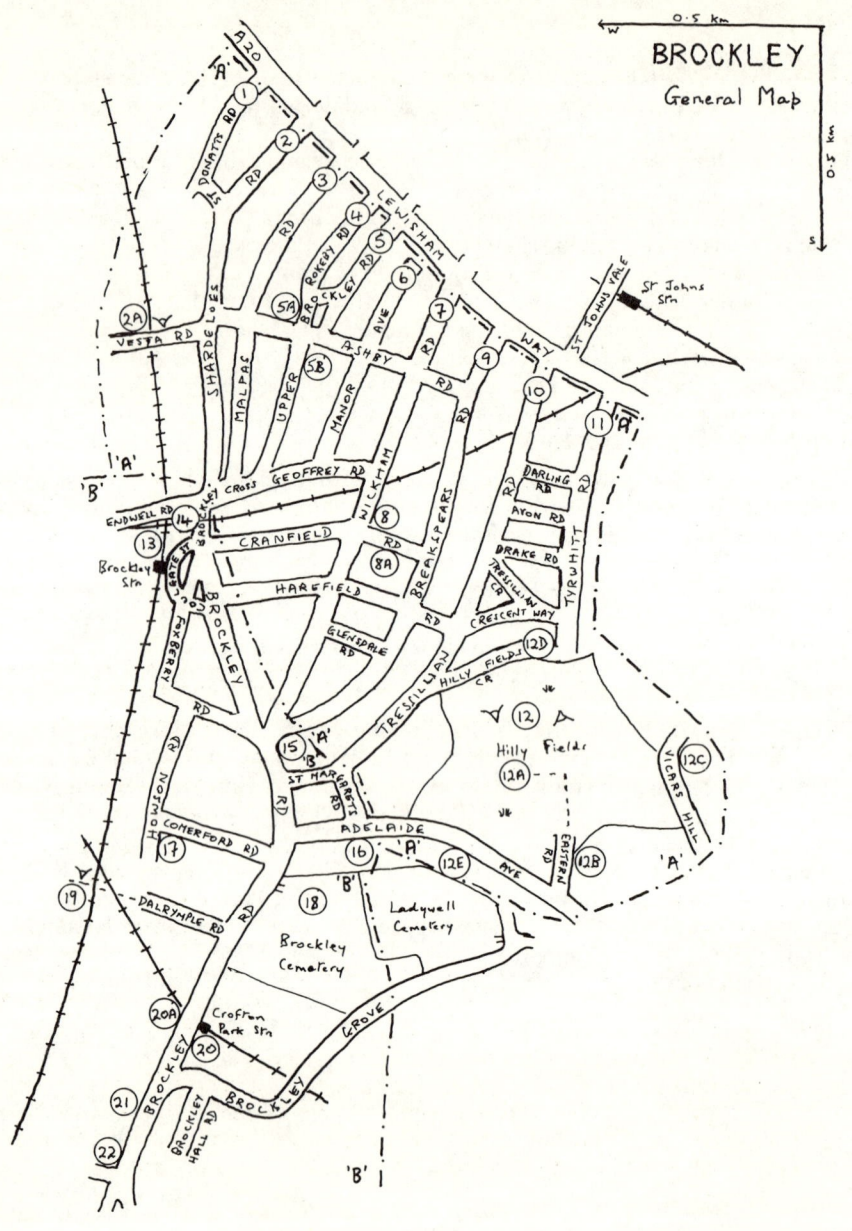

BROCKLEY

Gazetteer

Section 'A' UPPER BROCKLEY

1. St Donatts Road consists mainly of groups of the late 1850s, many on the west side in use by Goldsmiths College.

2. Shardeloes Road has some terraces of the 1850s to the north of the junction with St Donatts Road. The southern part of the road is the site of a section of the Croydon Canal which was not used when the Croydon Railway was laid down in 1839 *(see New Cross 1)*, and for this reason there are no houses here on the west side.

To the west, the wide modern iron **Vesta Road bridge (2A)** gives a wonderful view of the Croydon Railway in its wide and deep cutting.

3. Malpas Road has some long terraces of Italianate cottages of the 1850s. Nos 44/90 on the east side have a course below the upper floors of guilloche decoration, forming a very positive decorative feature. Opposite, **The Duke of Edinburgh**, no 81, is a pub of 1868. Further south the houses are late 19th century.

4. Rokeby Road has on the west side a long terrace of Italianate cottages of the 1850s, ending with a group of 1853 - no 37, a house with a fine loggia and ornamental railings, and two pairs, nos 38/39 and 41/42. On the east side, towards the north, note no 70, of 1853; no 73, of 1866; and nos 74/82, of 1934, a terrace of strange roughcast houses, with entrances projecting forward in polygonal porches at the head of flights of steps.

5. Upper Brockley Road is part of an old lane which was continued by Brockley Road beyond Brockley Cross to the original site of Brockley Green. At the northern end **nos 2/24** are fine pairs of 1850. The road veers westwards to **Brockley Baptist Church (5A)**, an elaborate Gothic church of 1867.

To the south is an area which has the atmosphere of an urban village - on the east side are **The Wickham Arms**, no 69, a pub of 1862, and nos 71/93, an attractive and unified shopping parade known as the **Forecourt (5B)**, of the late 1860s, restored c1968; on the west side are **Lord Wolseley**, no 76, a pub of 1868, and some nice Italianate terraces of the 1860s.

6. Manor Avenue, with the Memorial Gardens *(see Deptford 44A)* at its northern end, has a series of long and harmonious Italianate terraces of the early 1860s.

7. Wickham Road *(even numbers west side, odd numbers east side, starting from Lewisham Way)* was laid out c1850, and is the widest road in the area.

The earliest houses are on the west side. Nos 2/4 are of 1851, nos 6/8 of 1853, nos 10/12 of 1855, no 14 of 1856, and nos 16 and 18 of 1860, all Italianate though no 14 shows some Gothic influence. Development on the west side continued in Italianate style in the early 1860s to just beyond Ashby Road. Development further south shows mainly Gothic influence, though there are some Italianate houses. Note nos 28/30, a fine Italianate pair of 1870 with impressive porches; no 60, with its elegant iron balcony, of 1869; and nos 72/74, a large pair with all doors and windows in Gothic pointed style, of 1880.

The east side was developed to no 19 in the 1860s, nos 1/3 of 1861 and nos 5/9 of 1862 being fine Italianate houses, and as far as Harefield Road in the 1870s.

In **Glensdale Road**, a short road linking Wickham Road and Breakspears Road, note on the north side three nice pairs with pointed Gothic doorways and windows c1878, similar to 72/74 Wickham Road.

8. *St Peters Church, Wickham Road. A very large stone Gothic church by Frederick Marrable of 1868. The west frontage with its three doorways is very impressive, but the tower owes its grandeur largely to the castellated octagon added by Sir Arthur Blomfield in 1891.

The **interior** *(contact the vicarage next door, or ring 0181-691 3334)* is imposing, though the profusion of stained glass (added, mostly by Clayton & Bell, after 1870, and not part of the architect's concept) makes it seem rather gloomy. The nave is very wide with great Gothic arches covering the aisles as well; it is of light red brick with bright red brick dressings over the arches. The chancel is vaulted, of polychrome brick, with a fine pattern of mosaics and tiles in the apsidal east end. There are two Gothic pulpits, and a fine marble font at the west end, spoilt by a later fussy wooden cover.

In Cranfield Road to the south is **St Peters Centre (8A)**, the church hall, a Gothic building of 1878.

9. Breakspears Road *(even numbers west side, odd numbers east side, starting from Lewisham Way)* was developed on the west side as far as Ashby Road with two imposing Italianate terraces, nos 2/8 of 1868 and nos 10/16 of 1869. Development at the southern end was in the 1870s, and in the middle section in the 1880s; the houses were mostly with Gothic influences and decoration, though there are some houses with round-headed doorways in a more Italianate style.

The east side was not developed until the 1880s, and has some interesting houses. The first group, nos 13/21 of 1885, are imposing detached houses with fine decoration, quite riotous in the case of nos 19/21. Much further south, as the road curves, there are two finely decorated pairs - nos 109/111 of 1885 with a grand paired porch, and nos 133/5 of 1880 with extravagant decoration.

10. Tressillian Road *(even numbers west side, odd numbers east side, starting from Lewisham Way)* was developed as far south as Darling Road c1868, and these houses show the beginnings of Gothic influences. Development further south was in the 1870s, and particularly from Avon Road onwards, the houses become more Gothic and have more fanciful decoration and ornamental flourishes. Nos 49/51 are handsome highly ornamented houses c1875 with Gothic doorcases; nos 50/94, of the late 1870s, form a sequence of imposing gabled houses. Beyond Drake Road are some very grand houses with Gothic doorcases and distinguished decorative features - note no 69, and nos 96 and 98 (which has an amazing row of seven first floor windows), all c1879.

The short roads which link Tressillian Road and Tyrwhitt Road all have interesting houses:

Darling Road was developed in the late 1860s, some houses having strange doorcase capitals, fine gables, and fanciful decorative features.

Avon Road was developed from 1873. Many houses have extraordinary decorated plasterwork on the upper floor, particularly nos 9/11 and 10/12.

Drake Road was developed in the 1870s, consisting of gabled pairs with strange capitals in recessed porches, forming an appealing pattern.

Tressillian Crescent was developed in the 1870s, and has houses with Gothic influences, as well as a group c1974 which fits in well. Note in particular no 2, a large and imposing house with a fine location facing down Tressillian Road; no 6, with a LCC blue plaque 'Edgar Wallace writer 1875-1932 lived here' (many of his 170 novels are set in Deptford and Greenwich); no 12, with a Gothic pointed doorway.

Crescent Way was developed in the 1870s, and includes gabled pairs with Gothic capitals, as well as imposing pairs (like those in a nearby part of Tyrwhitt Road) with gabled end bays and long lower sections in between. At the western end is Tower House, a detached house with a tower, of red brick (virtually unique in this predominantly stock brick area), riotously decorated.

11. Tyrwhitt Road *(even numbers west side, odd numbers east side, starting from Lewisham Way)* was developed from 1859. **The Talbot**, no 2, the handsome classical pub at the northern end of the street, is of 1868. No 1 of 1859 and no 8 of 1862 both have handsome classical porches. Nos 10/28 are Italianate houses and nos 3/49 Italianate terraces built between 1859 and c1865, all well designed. During the late 1860s development continued in Italianate style southwards to around the Avon Road junction, where Gothic influences begin to appear, particularly in the doorcase capitals, some of which are quite strange. Similar features continued southwards on the east side in the late 1860s, whilst on the west side, as far as Tressillian Crescent, is a long and imposing sequence of pairs with gabled end bays and long lower sections in between, of the early 1870s. The street ends at Hilly Fields, with substantial detached houses opposite each other, no 102 c1879 and no 105 c1877.

12. *Hilly Fields. The top, 50 metres high, of this large grassed area with steep sides, provides fantastic panoramic *views, though some views towards Central and East London are blocked by tall trees, particularly in the summer.

Hilly Fields became a park in 1896, preserving it from future development; by this time the school which dominates it was already there. West Kent Grammar School was built on a high point almost in the centre in 1885. After it closed, the building was acquired by the London County Council in 1907 for Brockley County School, and large and prominent extensions followed. The building was taken over in 1995 by **Prendergast School (12A)**, moving here from Catford.

The oldest part is to the north, in vaguely Jacobean style with a grand projecting entrance bay. The extensions to the south of 1913 and 1921 are larger, in similar red brick but rather more formal, except for the assembly hall of 1913 to the east, with its great traceried east window.

The interior of the *Assembly Hall is fascinating, containing a remarkable series of murals of 1933-36 as well as fine stained glass of 1890.

The murals are in three large panels on the north wall and two on the south wall, and on and under the gallery at the west end. The artists were students at the Royal College of Art, and the style picturesque, idealised and romantic, much influenced by Stanley Spencer. The panels on the north wall are: 'Fortune and the Boy at the Well' by Charles Mahoney, 'Joy and Sorrow' by Charles Mahoney, and 'The Country Girl and the Milk Pail' by Evelyn Dunbar. The panels on the south wall are: 'The Bird Catcher and the Skylark' by Mildred Eldridge, and 'The King and two Shepherds' by Violet Martin. Along the front of the gallery is a long mural 'Hilly Fields' by Evelyn Dunbar, featuring Hilly Fields with the school in the centre, allegorical figures at either end (one holding a plan of the school and the other a plan of Hilly Fields), and two panels above with schoolboys in rugby clothes and school uniform. Under the gallery, the lunettes and spandrels are covered in murals by Evelyn Dunbar, some based on Aesop's Fables, and the ceiling in murals by Charles Mahoney, the central one including trompe l'oeil plasterwork and roundels of bonneted figures.

Also in the hall are four tall illuminated stained glass panels of 1890 brought from the old Prendergast school at Catford - on the north wall male allegorical figures representing Art and Science, and on the south wall female allegorical figures representing Music and Dancing.

If you have a special interest in viewing the murals and stained glass in the Assembly Hall, contact the School by post or on 0181-690 3710 to request an appointment.

The school is accessed by Eastern Road, off Adelaide Avenue. **21 Eastern Road (12B)** has a Lewisham Council plaque: 'Henry Williamson, writer, 1895-1977, lived here 1902-20'; he is best known as the author of 'Tarka the Otter' and other nature stories.

Note also three modern Prendergast School buildings below on Adelaide Avenue - to the left the gymnasium of 1995 parallel with the road, then the science block of the 1960s, enlarged 1995, and further right, the low-lying exams block of 1997.

The roads fringing Hilly Fields have several fanciful buildings of c1900. **46/56 Vicars Hill (12C)** form a fine group - Copperfield, no 46, an arts and crafts house notable for the continuous band of windows along the ground floor, with an oriel and a projecting bay window above; nos 48/50 and 52/54, pairs with elaborate friezes, strange porches, and oriels in the gable; and Kent Lodge, no 56, with a fancifully decorated porch and a dragon figure at the top. **1/4 Hilly Fields Crescent (12D)** are two pairs with balconies supported on columns, looking like an extended terrace in the view from the hill.

On the front of **82 & 86 Adelaide Avenue (12E)** are two small **Bridge House Estate** property marks. (There is another such mark at 135 Ladywell Road - *see Lewisham 40.*)

> The income from the Bridge House Estate paid for and maintains the four bridges owned by the Corporation of London - London Bridge, Blackfriars Bridge, Southwark Bridge, Tower Bridge. The estate originated with a bequest for the upkeep of the old London Bridge completed in 1201, the other bridges of course being much later. There are a number of Bridge House properties in Deptford and on the Brockley / Ladywell border, but most of the property marks are no longer there.

BROCKLEY

Gazetteer

Section 'B' BROCKLEY CROSS to CROFTON PARK
(See map on page 62)

13. Brockley Station opened in 1871 on the Croydon Railway. Now there is just a small basic building of 1991, leading down to platforms in a cutting. An iron footbridge of 1995 crosses the line, linking Coulgate Street and Mantle Road; from here can be seen three other iron bridges in close proximity - a footbridge linking the platforms, a railway bridge carrying the Nunhead Loop Line, and a modern road bridge carrying Endwell Road over the Croydon Railway at Brockley Cross.

In **Coulgate Street** opposite the station, **nos 1 (part), 2, 2a,** and **3** are a group of four cottages of 1833 - note the continuous roofline. These cottages once faced the Croydon Canal, which was used for the Croydon Railway from this point southwards.

Also in Coulgate Street note a series of murals 1991-93 showing aspects of Brockley life, topped by a mural of Brockley Lane Station; these were organised by the Brockley Society, and carried out by local artists.

Nearby, at the junction of Brockley Road and Foxberry Road, is **Breakspeare Arms**, a large pub of the 1860s, with an attractive projecting rounded ground floor front; now disused, it is due for restoration.

14. 28a Brockley Cross, a secondhand furniture shop, was the booking-hall of the former **Brockley Lane Station**, much altered and with a new roof; the station opened 1872 on the Greenwich Park Line. Opposite, **11 Brockley Cross** is a spiky house of 1872, originally the stationmasters house. *See also Lewisham 31.*

> TheGreenwich Park Line ran from Nunhead via Brockley Lane and Lewisham Road Stations to Blackheath Hill from 1871, and was extended to Greenwich Park 1888; it closed in 1917. In 1929 part of the line was re-opened to form the Nunhead Loop Line for freight. This line was brought into use for passengers in 1935, and is now used for the service from Lewisham to Victoria.

15. St Andrews Church, Brockley Road. This large Gothic church with its tall stone spire was built 1882 for the Presbyterian Church of England; since c1975 it has been Brockley United Reformed Church. The design of the ornate west double doorways with three elongated Gothic windows above was based on Jedburgh Abbey (in the Scottish borders). The interior *(contact 0181-691 2021)* has a fine wooden gallery all around, with iron columns going through the gallery to form great Gothic arches and support the roof. Behind the altar is a fine wooden pulpit.

68 - BROCKLEY

16. St Margarets Square consists of a unified terrace of houses, set back from Adelaide Avenue behind an enclosed green. The houses, c1886, are distinctive, multi-gabled and intricately designed. There are similar houses nearby in Adelaide Avenue.

St Margarets Road opposite has a number of extraordinary tall houses of the early 1880s with densely packed gables and nice patterns incised in the plasterwork.

17. St Mary Magdalens Church, Howson Road, a pleasing Roman Catholic red brick church of 1899 with twin front cupolas, restored and extended in the 1940s; the interior is also pleasing, with an elliptical arch to the chancel. The adjacent St Mary Magdalens School is of 1895.

18. Brockley Cemetery was opened in 1858 as Deptford Cemetery; a wall divided it from Lewisham Cemetery, now Ladywell Cemetery *(see Lewisham 41)*, to the east which opened the same year. They were merged in 1965, the wall being replaced by a grassed ridge planted with a line of trees. The main entrance is now at the Ladywell end, but there is a pedestrian entrance at the Brockley end.

The Brockley part has some lovely tree-lined avenues, otherwise there is little landscape interest. The most interesting feature is an L-shaped group of large monuments on tiled plinths, densely packed together near the entrance.

Margaret and Rachel McMillan *(see Deptford 19)* were buried here; from the entrance, take the path to the right parallel with Brockley Road, and their granite headstone is a short distance along on the right - Rachel McMillan died 1917, her sister Margaret McMillan 1931.

By a hedge almost opposite the Brockley Cemetery entrance is a short iron post, a property mark of Christs Hospital 1807.

19. Dalrymple Road bridge is mainly a modern iron footbridge over the Croydon Railway, which is in a wide deep cutting, the former route of the Croydon Canal; but the eastern part is older and of brick, crossing the Catford Loop Line *(see below)* which itself has a modern iron bridge going over the Croydon Railway to the north.

20. Crofton Park Station. The original handsome red brick station building of 1892 remains, with covered walkways leading down to the canopied platforms. This is on the Catford Loop Line from Nunhead to Shortlands, which opened 1892.

On the other side of the railway line is **Crofton Park Library**, a baroque building of 1905, with an Ionic porch and a fanciful Dutch gable.

The **Rivoli Ballroom (20A)** opposite was originally a cinema, Crofton Park Picture Palace, of 1913, substantially extended 1924.

21. Brockley Jack, 410 Brockley Road. A large and splendid pub of 1898 with lots of fanciful features; it is on the site of an 18th century pub. It incorporates a theatre. Inside, on the wall in the front bay, is an old inn sign made from the shoulder-blade of a whale, and said to be from the time of the original pub; a representation of the sign in stone is outside on the front at the top of the tall gable.

22. Church of St Hilda, Brockley Road. The parish church of Crofton Park, a strange Arts and Crafts church of 1908 by Greenaway & Newberry. Note the semi-circular traceried windows, looking truncated, and the stumpy tower topped by an octagonal parapet with a chequer pattern. The interior *(contact the Vicarage, Buckthorne Road, 0181-699 1277)* is lofty with widely spaced Gothic arcades.

LEWISHAM

Introduction

Lewisham is a suburban town centred on Lewisham High Street, a long shopping street which extends one and a half kilometres from near Lewisham Station in the north to Rushey Green, the shopping centre of Catford, in the south. It lies in the valley of the River Ravensbourne, which runs to the west of the High Street throughout.

The River Ravensbourne rises at the ponds on Keston Common, and flows through Bromley and Beckenham Place Park before reaching Ladywell and Lewisham. It then continues through Brookmill Park to Deptford Bridge, and beyond this point it becomes Deptford Creek and is tidal and navigable on its way to the Thames.

The Ravensbourne is joined by its tributary the River Quaggy near Lewisham Station. The River Quaggy rises at Petts Wood (where it is also called the Kyd Brook), then flows through Sundridge Park, Grove Park (where it is also called the Chin Brook) and Lee, and runs to the south of Lee High Road before reaching the Lewisham town centre.

Early history

The Saxon manor of Lewisham (first mentioned in a charter of 862) was very large, covering Greenwich and Woolwich as well; it remained a royal manor until 1624. The original village was close to St Mary's Church, the original parish church of Lewisham, which dates back to at least 1100.

There were several mills on the Ravensbourne, the most important being the Armoury Mill (near Lewisham Station), which was established by the 14th century; it ground steel for Henry VIII's armoury at the Palace of Placentia at Greenwich, and continued this work for royal armouries up to c1637.

Georgian Lewisham

By the 17th century a number of houses, large and small, had appeared here and there along the High Street.

By the end of the 18th century Lewisham had become a very long village, with several quite large houses. Apart from the old Vicarage and the former Brooklands House, the larger houses have gone, though the upper floors of some of the smaller houses have survived above present-day shops. A stream ran the full length of the High Street; its route is indicated by the grassed strips outside Lewisham Hospital.

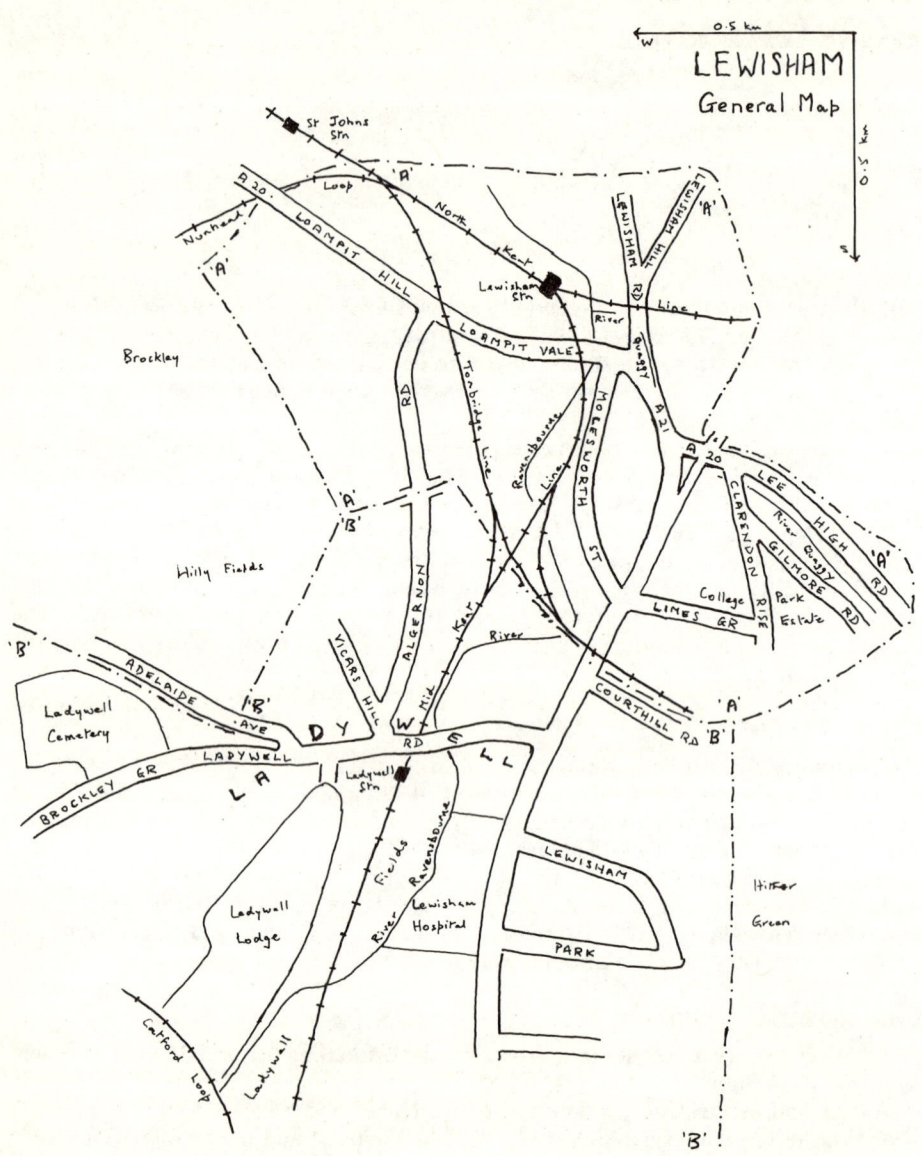

Brick-making and quarrying had by c1790 become established to the west of Lewisham Bridge, south of Loampit Vale and Loampit Hill. The mills on the Ravensbourne were mainly corn-mills, though the Riverdale Mill (the only mill which has survived) was involved in leather manufacture for much of the 18th century. The old Armoury Mill had a variety of uses until it became the Royal Small Arms Factory from 1807 to 1818; later it became the Lewisham Silk Mills, and the buildings were finally demolished in 1937.

The old village green of Lewisham, Watch House Green, situated between the High Street and Lewis Grove, was enclosed c1815, as was Plough Green, at the northern corner of the High Street and Loampit Vale, where there had been an annual fair. Little has survived from the early 19th century, except for Camden Villas in the High Street and a few houses in George Lane.

The coming of the railways

The opening of Deptford Station in 1836 heralded the railway age, though this may have been too far away to have a direct impact. But by the time Lewisham Station opened in 1849, housing development had already begun in streets off the High Street, and in the 1840s groups of purpose-built shops appeared in the High Street, marking the start of the shopping centre we know today.

The first Lewisham Station of 1849 was on the North Kent Line; in 1857 it was moved slightly west to form a junction with the Mid Kent Line. A tremendous growth in housing then followed, and the grounds of many large houses and farms were developed. Many streets to the east of the High Street retain the character of this period, particularly around St Stephens Church and on the College Park Estate. Two fine terraces of the period have survived on either side of the North Kent Line railway bridge, as well as an enclave at the beginning of Silk Mills Path. A unique development of large houses began further south at Lewisham Park, but only one of these houses has survived. There are a number of survivals in Eastdown Park, which was an isolated development off Lee High Road.

In 1855 sewerage works led to the draining of the stream along the High Street; 'if it is possible to point to any one moment at which Lewisham ceased to be a village, this is that moment' (John Coulter).

Ladywell

The same sewerage works of 1855 also led to the disappearance of two springs in the area of Ladywell, which, though it is close to the churchyard of St Mary's and to Lewisham High Street, now has quite a distinct identity. There had been, at least since the 15th century, a Holy Well, located near where the present Ladywell Bridge crosses the railway line. Also, by the end of the 18th century, a mineral spring had appeared further west.

Ladywell began to develop c1780, but its present village character is largely due to the terraced cottages which followed the opening of Ladywell Station in 1857, and to the fields alongside the River Ravensbourne. Ladywell Road and Brockley Grove follow the route of the old lane linking Lewisham with Brockley.

At the eastern end of Ladywell Road is a remarkable sequence of late 19th century municipal buildings - two in Gothic style, and two in Queen Anne style - in varying shades of red brick.

Fanciful late Victorian housing

The housing of the mid 19th century which followed the arrival of the railways was predominantly in Italianate style. But from the 1870s Gothic influences became dominant, and many surviving terraces and groups display fanciful and often quite extravagant decorative features. This style, at its best in the streets of Upper Brockley *(see Brockley Introduction, page 61)*, extends into neighbouring parts of Lewisham - in and around Loampit Hill, and in several streets in Ladywell around the junction of Vicars Hill and Algernon Road. A series of houses in similar style can be seen in Mount Pleasant Road, to the east of the High Street.

Lewisham 2000

The shopping centre continued to grow. In 1884 Chiesmans department store (which became Army & Navy in 1976) was set up, and with its extension of 1914, became a very large store. The adjoining Co-op store opened in 1933, and by this time Lewisham was challenging Woolwich as the premier shopping centre in the region. (Both stores have now gone - the Co-op closed c1983 and its ground floor is now Yates's Wine Lodge, the Army & Navy closed 1994 and its two sites have been empty since 1996.)

Although the Lewisham Centre had opened in 1975, it was clear during the 1980s that the centres at Bromley and Bexleyheath were growing faster, and that High Street traffic was making shopping rather unpleasant.

This led to the setting up of Lewisham 2000, a largescale town centre improvement scheme, which started in 1992 and was completed by 1995. The main shopping centre is now by-passed and largely pedestrianised, the Lewisham Centre has been upgraded, and the shopping environment has been much improved. There is a lot of imaginative street furniture.

However, the northern part is currently really desolate, with traffic on the A20 still pouring through. This part is characterised by the featureless open space of the great roundabout and the uninspired Quaggy Gardens, by the harsh concrete channels of the two rivers, and by several large empty sites - the two empty sites of the Army & Navy Store, the derelict Odeon cinema site opposite the roundabout, and another empty site on the other side of Molesworth Street. All this sets up a physical and psychological barrier when one arrives at the Railtrack, Docklands Light Railway and bus stations. From here the town centre seems remote, and the Lewisham Centre and the Citibank Tower looming above look bleak and obtrusive.

When the environment of the northern approach is improved, the Lewisham town centre may develop an overall appeal. But at the time of writing this seems a long way off. The Odeon site may be developed with a new leisure complex by 1999, but there seems little prospect of development of the Army & Navy sites (now owned by the Metropolitan Police) being completed before 2002.

LEWISHAM

Gazetteer

Section 'A' LEWISHAM NORTH & LOAMPIT VALE
(See map on page 74)

1. Lewisham Station. This is the second station, built 1857, restored 1983. Note the finely carved iron columns under the front canopy and on the up platform of the line from Blackheath.
> The first Lewisham Station was opened on the North Kent Line (to Strood via Blackheath) in 1849; it was located over the tracks just east of the High Street. The station was moved to its present site in 1857 as the junction station for the North Kent Line and the Mid Kent Line (to Beckenham via Ladywell), and was called Lewisham Junction until 1929. The new Lewisham Station of the Docklands Light Railway will be opened opposite by the year 2000.

2. Lewisham Bus Station, opened 1994, at present a large open space, but about to be transformed with the opening of the Docklands Light Railway station on part of the site by the year 2000. The main station building will occupy the site of the Mid Kent Tavern, a pub of c1862 with distinctive ornamental features, shortly to be demolished.

The River Ravensbourne flows underneath before being joined by the River Quaggy on the north side of the site. On the south side is **Lewisham Bridge (2A)**, over the Ravensbourne; it was last rebuilt in 1993 - the first stone bridge here was medieval.

The Plough (2B), 2 Lewisham High Street, now called Pitchers, an impressive pub of 1849, remains on the edge of the site.

3. Silk Mills Path. This footpath, which starts at the railway viaduct in Lewisham Road, first passes an attractive enclave of Italianate houses, **nos 1/6** (three pairs) and **Sharsted Villas** (one pair), of the 1850s. It continues between the River Ravensbourne and the Tesco store, and then crosses the Tesco car park and emerges on Conington Road; to the left are the gateway piers (and part of the wall) of the former **Lewisham Silk Mills**, originally c1895, but restored and moved further apart after the war. This area will undergo considerable disruption during the construction of the Docklands Light Railway, and this may involve demolition of the gateway piers and wall.

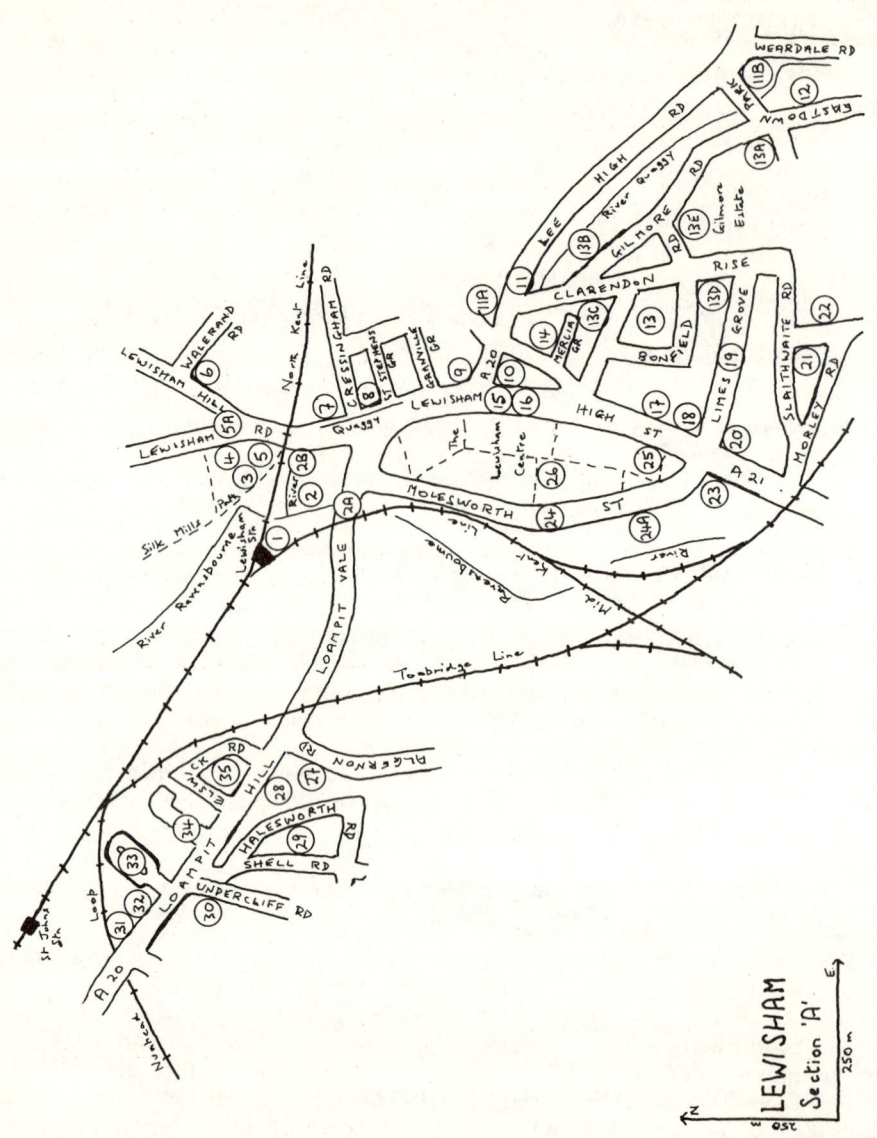

The Lewisham Silk Mills site was to the west of Silk Mills Path; it is now in part the Conington Industrial Estate and in part disused. The site was formerly the Armoury Mill, which was established by the 14th century; it ground steel for Henry VIII's armoury at the Palace of Placentia at Greenwich, and continued this work for royal armouries up to c1637. It then had a variety of uses until 1807, when it became the Royal Small Arms Factory; this closed in 1818. By 1825 the mill was used for silk throwing (converting raw silk into silk thread), and eventually became known as Lewisham Silk Mills, producing gold and silver thread. The mill produced wire only from 1930 to 1937, when the buildings were demolished.

4. Tesco Store. A sprawling but pleasant building in vernacular style, c1987.

On Lewisham Road, but within the site, is **Eagle House**, built c1870 as the office of Anchor Brewery (established here 1818). The brewery was taken over by Whitbreads in 1891 and became its first bottling plant, closing in 1984. Note the relief sculpture on the side wall, **The Picnic**, by Gerda Rubinstein 1988.

5. Heath Terrace, 292/306 Lewisham Road, a handsome Italianate terrace of 1854; an end house has a Tuscan porch, the others have Tuscan doorcases.

Opposite, at the junction with Lewisham Hill, is a Portland stone **obelisk (5A)**, originally with a drinking fountain, of 1866.

6. Walerand Road has, outside modern flats by the junction with Lewisham Hill, gate piers and part of the wall remaining from **Colfes School** of 1889 (which replaced the original building of 1652 on the site).

> Colfes School was founded in 1652 by Abraham Colfe, Vicar of Lewisham, and taken over by the Leathersellers Company after his death in 1657; it moved from this site to Horn Park Lane, Lee, in 1964. *(See also 56.)*

7. 17/31 Lewisham High Street, an attractive Italianate terrace c1864, with Ionic doorcases and stuccoed rusticated ground floors. **No 15** is however a pastiche addition of 1994 *(see below)*. Alongside, the River Quaggy makes a rare (though not particularly pleasant) appearance.

Kings Hall Mews leads behind to the head office of **Beaver Housing Association**. Built 1994, it has a post-modernist circular glazed entrance hall. Beyond is Drovers Court, more traditional, part of the same project. Also in 1994, 15 Lewisham High Street was added to the terrace in front in authentic matching style.

8. Church of St Stephen. This Victorian Gothic ragstone church of 1865 by Sir George Gilbert Scott looks uninspired and unfinished. In fact, the tower and spire intended over the north transept was not built, as the ground was found to be too marshy. The west end has tall lancets and a wheel window; the south transept has twin gables.

The ***interior** is much more interesting, and in fact quite splendid. *(The church is often open Wednesdays at noon, and on Thursdays the front doors are normally open, allowing a not very satisfactory view of the interior through a glass screen; otherwise contact 0181-318 1295.)* The arcades are impressive, with a variety of foliated capitals. But the dominant features are the dramatic rood screen by Frank Harding 1916, and at the west end, the great organ gallery of 1941 by Sir Charles Nicholson. Bright stained glass windows in the chancel and the Lady Chapel are by J. E. Nuttgens 1954; a number of intriguing stained glass medallions by Clayton & Bell survived war damage and are in the wheel window and other windows. Note also the reredos of the Last Supper, of 1873.

The former **Vicarage**, in Cressingham Road, is angular and unusual, of 1874.

The church is in an attractive enclave consisting mainly of terraced Italianate houses, in particular in **St Stephens Grove** and **Granville Grove**, of the 1860s, but also in parts of **Cressingham Road**, of the 1870s.

9. Yates's Wine Lodge, with its vast and jolly bar / lounge, opened 1995, occupies the ground floor of the old **Co-op Store**, which was known as Tower House. The store building was opened by the Royal Arsenal Co-operative Society in 1933; the other date on the front, 1868, was when the RACS was founded. The store closed c1983. The curved facade is quite striking with its central tower, art deco detail, and stone bas-relief featuring trains, ships, and a lorry marked RACS.

> The RACS was founded by workers at the Royal Arsenal, Woolwich, in 1868. The first shop was opened at 147 Powis Street, Woolwich, in 1873, and the RACS went on to become one of the largest retail co-ops in the country. Many services provided to its members were pioneering advances of the time, including low-cost housing, adult education, and libraries. The RACS was absorbed by the Manchester-based CWS (Co-operative Wholesale Society) in 1985.

10. 85/93 Lewisham High Street, a series of quite splendid bank buildings - Barclays Bank c1880, an extension of the 1930s with great columns, and Midland Bank c1898. They are the only prewar buildings surviving on the island site which was until the early 19th century Watch House Green, the village green of Lewisham.

11. Lee High Road. *This road, nearly two kilometres long, runs from the Lewisham Town Centre to Lee Green. The western part only, between Lewis Grove and Weardale Road, is featured here, going from west to east.*

The White Horse (11A), no 1, an early 19th century pub, rebuilt in Italianate style, probably in the 1860s.

The Sultan, no 14, an early 19th century pub, rebuilt probably in 1885.

Nos 18/54, a long one-storey balustraded parade of shops, built c1914.

Nos 66/78, part of an early 19th century terrace, there before 1814.

No 102, of 1813, a surviving part of a terrace.

Grove Cottage, no 138, a small building of 1835 with a fine doorcase, a strange survival in a stretch of the road largely devoted to car showrooms and workshops.

Rose of Lee (11B), no 162, now called Hobgoblin, a rather stately pub rebuilt c1897 with a clock in the central gable.

12. Eastdown Park was developed in the 1860s, when there were still fields all around; many attractive houses survive. Note **nos 15/17**, opposite the old telephone exchange, c1860, sharing a prominent gable; **no 45**, an impressive detached stuccoed Italianate house, c1865; and **nos 57/59**, an attractive stuccoed Italianate pair, c1860.

13. College Park Estate, around Gilmore Road, Clarendon Rise, Albion Way and Bonfield Road, was developed from 1868. Note:

At the junction of Gilmore Road with Eastdown Park is a former **Telephone Exchange (13A)**, an impressive neo-Georgian building of the 1900s by Leonard Stokes, of brick with stone pilasters, the top storey added later.

Outside is a **K6 red cast-iron telephone kiosk**, designed by Sir Giles Gilbert Scott in 1935. It is distinguishable from the K2 type in that it incorporates some narrow rectangular panes of glass. This is the only K6 kiosk remaining in the Deptford / Lewisham area, whereas there are many examples of the earlier K2, designed by Scott 1927, which has all panes of glass the same size.

9 Gilmore Road (13B), a house of 1871, has a GLC blue plaque to James Elroy Flecker, 1884-1915, poet and dramatist, who was born here.

College Park Baptist Church (13C), Clarendon Rise, a small building of 1874 with accentuated Gothic doors and windows.

Two remarkable buildings **(13D)** in **Clarendon Rise** connected with the former St Marks Church (built 1870, demolished 1969) survive; they were both designed by Greenaway & Newberry in 1914. **No 36** was the Vicarage, in arts & crafts style, with distinctive brickwork. Adjacent is the old **Church Hall**, now used by a printing firm, a distinctive Gothic building with a great east window.

Gilmore Estate (13E), a large and quite pleasing estate of 1979, with plum-brick houses and a lot of open space.

14. Mercia Grove is an attractive close with similar Italianate terraces of the early 1850s on both sides.

15. The Clock Tower, erected by public subscription to commemorate the diamond jubilee of Queen Victoria 1897, marks the beginning of the pedestrianised part of the High Street. It is a square tower of Portland stone, topped by a short spire and gilt crown. It was moved here in 1995 from a traffic island slightly to the east.

16. Lewisham Market, predominantly a fruit and vegetable market, operates daily except Sundays. There is no sense of intimacy, but it is the only lively feature in the central shopping area of the High Street, which is lined mostly by totally uninspired modern buildings.

Exceptions to this are the old Burtons upper floors of the 1930s opposite the Clock Tower; the exotic cream-coloured art deco of the old Woolworths upper floors next to the main entrance to the Lewisham Centre; and on the east side, the stately upper floors of the old Times Furnishing Company.

17. St Saviours Church, a red brick Roman Catholic church of 1909. The Ionic doorcase has a mosaic fanlight. A tall campanile topped by a figure of Christ the King was added in 1929; it links the church to the presbytery, also of 1929, making an impressive integrated group. The presbytery is in arts & crafts style with intriguing brickwork.

The church is normally open, otherwise telephone 0181-852 2490. The interior has a Byzantine style nave and a classical sanctuary, and is notable for the lavish use of coloured marble. The sanctuary has a baroque ceiling fresco of the Transfiguration c1916, a high altar of Carrara marble, a marble pulpit, and an ambulatory.

> The church and the adjacent 169/171 Lewisham High Street were built on the site of The Limes, an early 18th century house in large grounds, demolished 1894. John Wesley, the founder of Methodism, frequently stayed there for long periods in the mid 18th century; his colleague George Whitefield also stayed there. There is a plaque on no 171, a house of 1900, to commemorate The Limes.

18. Prudential Buildings, 187/197 Lewisham High Street, is a very stylish red brick block c1905, with classical motifs in terracotta. The upper floors form a unified composition, with a balustrade along the first floor.

In the mews behind, note **Limes Hall**, a building with interesting decorative features, probably c1910. The original entrance was in the mews, the present entrance is from Limes Grove. Since 1983 it has been **Lewisham Labour Club**; during the interwar period it was Lewisham Spiritualist Church.

19. Limes Grove was laid out in 1849, nos 8/22 being pairs of that date; further along are nos 24/30, two pairs, and nos 32/38, a terrace, probably c1860.

20. Lewisham Library. This pleasing modern building opened in 1994; it was converted from an old telephone exchange of c1968. Note on a ground floor wall a plaque of 1901 to Alfred the Great, 'Lord of the Manor of Lewisham' - he was not, this story is based on a forged charter of 918. *Open Mondays 1000-1700, Tuesdays & Thursdays 0900-2000, Wednesdays, Fridays, Saturdays 0900-1700.* The building's external lighting system was designed by Ron Haselden to create an ever changing sculptural effect.

On the second floor is a large Reference Library and the **Local Studies Centre** *(phone 0181-297 0682, open as above except closed Wednesdays).*

21. 16/22 Slaithwaite Road are a group of fantastic houses of c1900 with extravagant decoration; in particular, no 22 has an amazing corner tower. **Nos 2/14** are large detached Italianate houses of c1870.

22. 8 Lingards Road has a Lewisham Council plaque to Leland Lewis Duncan, 1862-1923, the Lewisham local historian, who lived here 1873-1923. It is part of a fine group of restrained detached houses of the 1870s.

23. Camden Place, 226/230 Lewisham High Street, three large villas of c1821. They are currently in a sadly derelict state, but it is hoped that they will be restored soon for mainly residential use, with a restaurant at no 228. They remain from a group of four, the other was demolished c1993 for the traffic roundabout.

Opposite, **203, 207, 209/211** and **219/221 Lewisham High Street** retain upper floors of c1850, much altered (except nos 209/211).

24. Molesworth Street, originally a short cul-de-sac from Loampit Vale laid out in the late 1850s, now a dual carriageway opened 1994 as the town centre by-pass. It has a unique central reservation consisting of wavy patterns of Portland stone, designed by John Maine. On the roundabout at the south end is **Ridgeway**, a large sculpture by John Maine 1995, the abstract shape of which aligns with the angle of the sun as it varies between winter and summer.

***Riverdale Mill (24A)**, the only one of the Ravensbourne mills to survive, is basically of c1830, restored and much altered; it has a weatherboarded lucarne or hoist-house, an undershot wooden water-wheel, and a pond, liberally stocked with fish. It was in use as a leather mill during the 18th and early 19th century, and later became a corn mill. It now forms part of a Citibank complex, together with

***Riverdale House**, a long and tall brick office block, by Sir Frederick Gibberd & Partners 1981; its irregular, jagged exterior is striking, with rectangular piers and curved staircase towers.

In the grassed area to the south is **Column**, a white geometrical sculpture by John Maine; beyond is a footbridge over the River Ravensbourne, which here is in a concrete channel and not particularly appealing.

25. Lewisham Model Market is a narrow market of lock-up stalls, with the atmosphere and intimacy lacking in the main market. Next to the entrance, **194 Lewisham High Street** is a surviving 18th century cottage.

26. The Lewisham Centre. This pedestrianised precinct parallels the central shopping area of the High Street, to which it is linked by two walkways and through many of the larger shops. It was completed 1975, and attractively refurbished 1991. The central walkway is spacious and light with a glazed roof supported by cables; note the gaping maws of animals which are used for refuse. The Centre is integrated with the **Citibank Tower**, a tall slab block with a blue glass entrance, also of 1975.

27. Bibleway Tabernacle, originally the **Church of the Transfiguration**, built 1882 by James Brooks. A tall and narrow red brick church, with a fleche on top where nave and chancel met. The east end, facing Algernon Road, is austere with a blank arcade and lancets on two levels above; the nave has larger windows.

The **interior** *(phone 0181-691 3805 or 850 2894)* was radically transformed in 1953 when a new floor was inserted for the Institute for the Deaf. The Bibleway Tabernacle took over the building in 1978. The main church is in the old nave now oriented to the west, and there is a chapel in the old chancel facing east. The old nave has massive round pillars under low arches along the nave, and a narrow arcade with thin columns along the north side. There is a fine wooden pulpit at the west end; it used to be at the east end on a great marble base which is still there in the chapel.

28. The Angel, 11 Loampit Hill, is an Italianate pub c1853; nos 13/15, the adjoining cottages, are of the same date.

29. Halesworth Road has on both sides a series of paired gabled houses of the late 1890s, most with triangular Gothic porches, all with interesting decorative features, similar to Sunninghill Terrace opposite. The prominent corner house, no 1, is particularly striking. Together with **Shell Road**, where the houses are of c1900 and have similar decorative patterns, it forms a dramatic enclave. . .

30. Loampit Gospel Hall, 2 Undercliff Road, is a strange building with Gothic arches on the ground floor and a battlemented roof. It was built 1901 for the Welsh Presbyterian Church; they moved to a new building in Lewisham Way in 1924 *(see Deptford 48)*.

31. The Old Station, an architectural salvage yard, incorporates the timber-framed booking hall of 1871 of the former **Lewisham Road Station**, which was on the Greenwich Park Line. It retains its original room pattern, with the ticket office immediately to the left of the entrance. *See also Brockley 14.*

The Greenwich Park Line ran from Nunhead via Brockley Lane and Lewisham Road Stations to Blackheath Hill from 1871, and was extended to Greenwich Park 1888; it closed in 1917. The Lewisham Road platforms were demolished in 1929, when part of the line was re-opened to form the Nunhead Loop Line for freight. This line was brought into use for passengers in 1935, and is now used for the service from Lewisham to Victoria.

Look over the north side of the railway bridge to see where the platforms were; there is no trace either of the footbridge which linked the platforms.

On the other side of the line is the stationmaster's house, 291 Lewisham Way (now part of Whidbourne Close), probably c1887.

32. 64/70 Loampit Hill. A fine group of the late 1850s, by the local architect Alfred Cross. Nos 64 and 70 are very impressive detached houses with positive classical features. They flank nos 66/68, a pair, also classical but with some decorative flourishes around the doorcases. Adjacent is:

No 62, formerly called **Beaufort Lodge**, built by Alfred Cross for himself in the late 1850s. This is an incredible extravaganza of red brick with darker brick patterns; the porch is amazing, and there is a tower with a pagoda-like roof. There are all sorts of eccentricities and extraordinary decorative patterns, and the effect is exaggerated by a more recent colour scheme.

33. *Somerset Gardens, an oval green with old trees and surrounded by fine houses, built 1860 by Alfred Cross. To the left is a terrace of seven houses with a pattern of projecting gabled bays and recessed sections containing the entrance and a loggia. At the end and to the right are six detached classical villas, each with five round-headed windows on the upper floor. On the left side of no 17 is a plaque to 'Cecil Hepworth, British film pioneer, born here 1874'.

34. Sunninghill Terrace, 38/42 and 44/52 Loampit Hill, two terraces of the early 1880s. These are substantial houses with Gothic doorcase capitals and much fanciful ornamentation. **Sunninghill Road**, emerging between the terraces, has long terraces of smaller houses with similar decoration.

35. 28 Elswick Road bears a Lewisham Council plaque: 'Edith Nesbit, 1858-1924, children's writer and poet, lived here 1882-85'. The house is probably of 1879.

> Edith Nesbit and her husband Hubert Bland, a founder of the Fabian Society, actually lived here 1880-86. She lived nearly all her life in South East London. She was born in Kennington, and moved to Elswick Road after her marriage in 1880. After 1886 they moved to several houses in Lee (5 Cambridge Drive being the only one still standing), before moving in 1894 to The Three Gables, Baring Road, Grove Park, a larger house, now demolished.
>
> In 1899 they moved to Well Hall at Eltham, an early 18th century mansion with a moat behind which had enclosed the Tudor mansion of Well Hall. Most of Edith Nesbit's important work, including 'The Railway Children', was written there. Hubert Bland died in 1914; in 1917 she married Thomas 'Skipper' Tucker, Captain of the Woolwich Ferry. In 1922 they left Well Hall for St Marys in the Marsh, near Dymchurch, where she died; she is buried in the churchyard there. Well Hall was badly damaged by fire 1926, and demolished 1930; the site now forms part of the grounds of Well Hall Pleasaunce.

LEWISHAM

Gazetteer

Section 'B' LADYWELL & LEWISHAM SOUTH
(See map on page 82)

36. Ladywell Station was opened in 1857, when the Mid Kent Line was laid down from Lewisham to Beckenham. The original station building has largely survived on the up (west) side. The iron bridge linking the platforms was added later in the 19th century. By the entrance to the station is a Victorian wall letter-box.

37. Ladywell Bridge is in two parts, over the railway and over the river. The present bridge is of 1938. The first road bridge over the river was constructed in 1830; this was extended to cover the railway when it was laid down in 1857.

> The **Holy Well,** or Well of Our Lady, was located near where Ladywell Bridge crosses the railway. The well was there by 1472, and could have been much earlier; the name Lady Well appears on a map of 1592. Coping stones from the Holy Well were preserved for a long time in the garden of the former Ladywell Baths, but are now in store; it is planned to re-erect them in Ladywell Nature Reserve, which runs to the south of the station building on the down side. The well ran dry after construction of a sewer in 1855 *(see Introduction, page 71)*.
>
> The Holy Well is not to be confused with the Ladywell Mineral Spring, which was further west *(see 40)*; it also ran dry after the construction of the sewer in 1855.

38. Ladywell Village. By the railway is **Freemasons Arms**, 38 Ladywell Road, a pub of c1866. It forms part of a unified group of the mid 1860s, characterised by triplets of round-headed windows, extending up to no 52.

Further west are the oldest cottages in the Village - nos 74/76, a pair, and no 78, a larger house, all probably of the 1830s. Adjacent, **Ladywell Tavern**, no 80, is basically a building c1846, but substantially altered c1895 and at other times.

To the east, on the north side, are two Italianate terraces of 1857, interrupted by **Church Grove (38A)**, which has rather more attractive Italianate terraces facing each other, also of 1857.

39. Ladywell Lodge. Opened as a workhouse (for the aged and infirm poor) by Bermondsey Union 1900, it covered a vast site, which now falls into two separate parts, though there is a footpath link between them.

The original **gateway (39A)** of four red brick pillars remains at the end of Slagrove Place. To the left is the old porter's lodge, and further left the old stable block, now Ladywell Lodge Training Centre, both of 1900. Then follows **Slagrove Place Estate**, of 1995, facing a large green, and on the site of the old nursery block.

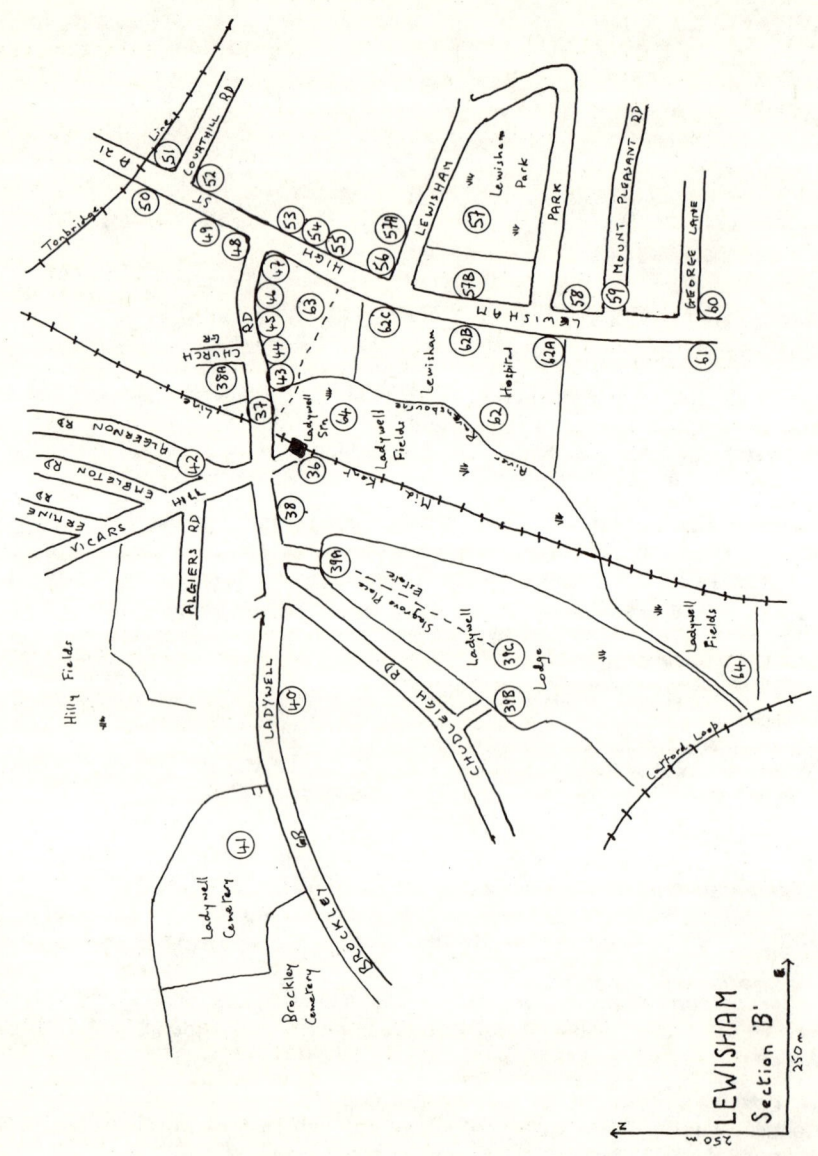

The other part of the site is reached along Chudleigh Road, then into Dressington Avenue, an estate of 1981. First you come to the **Water Tower (39B)**, a 37 metres high square tower, topped by a pavilion roof. Beyond, the east part of the **central admin block (39C)** of Ladywell Lodge has also survived from 1900. The old dining-hall with its cupola is now occupied by John Evelyn Education Centre; behind are two impressive pavilion blocks with polygonal corner towers, both now residential - looking from the east, the block to the left was the admin office, the block to the right the superintendent's house.

To the north are attractive modern buildings c1976, used by the Education Centre and by the Ladywell Centre. A green leads down to Ladywell Fields *(see 64)*.

40. 148 Ladywell Road, a house of c1900, has a Lewisham Council plaque: 'Site of the **Ladywell Mineral Spring** used for medicinal purposes until the mid 19th century'. Ladywell Spa was there by 1790, but ran dry after the construction of a sewer in 1855. Almost opposite, no 135, of the late 1880s, has a Bridge House Estate property mark *(see Brockley 12E)*; it is the smaller of the two marks.

41. Ladywell Cemetery was opened as Lewisham Cemetery in 1858; a wall divided it from Deptford Cemetery, now Brockley Cemetery *(see Brockley 18)*, to the east. They were merged in 1965, the wall being replaced by a grassed ridge planted with a line of trees. The main entrance is now at the Ladywell end and has imaginatively designed iron gates; an original gothic chapel survives nearby.

42. Algernon Road has, south of Ellerdale Street, long ranges of houses with fanciful and intricate decoration, of the 1880s and 1890s.

There are similar houses in Embleton Road, Ermine Road, Algiers Road, and towards the bottom of Vicars Hill, built during the same period.

43. St Mary's Centre, a very Gothic building of 1891, originally St Mary's Church Hall. Modern extension to the right, of 1988.

44. *Former Ladywell Baths, now Ladywell Gymnastics Club, a building of 1884 in deep red brick, notable for its great Gothic arches and the remarkable protruding circular tower, which has lost its cap.

45. Lewisham Coroners Court. A fanciful Gothic red brick building of 1894 with a grand entrance in Tudor style.

46. Lewisham Police Station. A nice Queen Anne style building in red brick of 1899, with a bowed section to the right, battlemented entrance porch, and a rounded projecting section on the left corner.

47. Former Lewisham Fire Station, in pleasing light red brick, of 1898. The main facade along Lewisham High Street is stately with four great round-headed arches separated by pilasters. The practice tower, tall and circular with a cone on top, is a prominent and dramatic landmark, best seen from the yard of the police station. The complex was converted for housing purposes in 1968.

48. *Ladywell House, formerly St Mary's Vicarage, recently well restored and now the offices of a security firm. This dignified and harmonious house was built 1693 for Dean George Stanhope *(see New Cross 33)*, and has a fine pedimented doorcase. The windows retain wooden mullions and transoms. The interior has an original staircase.

The house has been much extended, in a sympathetic style - to the rear by Edwin Nash in 1881, and to the west in 1895. The car park further along Ladywell Road provides a view of the rear extension, the fine garden, and of the stone doorway removed from the church tower in 1907 *(see 63)* and set into the garden wall to the right of the buildings.

49. 286/324 Lewisham High Street, an interesting group. **Nos 318/324** are two large pairs of 1904, and quite extravagant. **The Black Bull**, no 316, now known as The Fox and Firkin, has a rather jolly facade of 1907. **Nos 300/314** is basically an 18th century terrace, though altered in the late 19th century and with modern shopfronts. **The Castle**, no 286, a nice pub rebuilt c1890, with a castle in the gable.

50. 270/272 Lewisham High Street was once **Brooklands House**, a mansion c1782; the ground floor is now a furniture shop, but the upper floors are relatively unaltered, though not in good condition. The rear has twin bow windows to the ground floor.

51. Jasmine Bingo Club, Lewisham High Street. This is a bizarre edifice, built 1911 as a temperance billiard room and restaurant called Gild Hall. Faced in roughcast and painted blue, it displays an amazing mix of architectural features, including a domed centre, bowed windows, festoons, corner turrets, and Ionic columns.

52. Lewisham United Reformed Church, a very large Gothic ragstone church of 1867, with a soaring landmark spire. It was formerly Lewisham Congregational Church. The interior was destroyed during the last war; a new roof was inserted in 1957, cutting off the view of the upper part. Adjoining at the rear is the **Sunday School** of 1880, in similar style, now the church hall.

53. H. E. Olby, 299/313 Lewisham High Street, builders merchants, occupies a group of interesting buildings. No 299 is a pair of 1791 with a mansard roof. No 305 is impressively solid, c1876. Nos 307/313 is a modern block, probably of the late 1930s, with decorative mosaic tiling by the entrance.

54. 315/317 Lewisham High Street, the oldest shops in the High Street, originally a house probably c1700, with twin roofs, dormer windows, and a large chimney. But the effect is spoiled by the modern shopfronts, and the mid 19th century projecting upper floor on no 317.

55. *St Mary's School. This is an interesting complex, incorporating the oldest surviving school building in the Lewisham area, and retaining the appearance of a rural school. The building on the right with twin roofs is basically the original St Mary's National School of 1833, but considerably altered and extended in 1860 when it was divided into the boys school to the right and the girls school to the left. Behind is a modern block of 1975. The building on the left is of 1860, originally consisting of the teacher's house, projecting to the south, and the infant school, alongside Romborough Way; this building was extended later both to the west and to the east. It has a tower, great gables, Gothic doorways and lancet windows; an attractive group of stepped Gothic windows is visible from the car park in Romborough Way.

56. Colfe and Hatcliffe Glebe, 347 Lewisham High Street. A pleasing red brick building of 1952, situated opposite the site of the original Colfes Almshouses. It is the successor of both Colfes and Hatcliffes Almshouses.

Abraham Colfe was Vicar of Lewisham from 1610 to 1657. He founded Colfes Grammar School (which was intended for the children of 'ordinary people') at Lewisham Hill in 1652 with a bequest from a previous vicar John Glyn; it was taken over by the Leathersellers Company after his death in 1657 *(see also 6)*.

Colfes Almshouses were built c1665 by the Leathersellers Company with a bequest from Colfe; they were badly damaged during the war in 1944 and demolished in 1958, the Registrar's Office now occupying the site.

William Hatcliffe died in 1620; he left land for the poor of Greenwich and Lewisham. Almshouses were built at Catford Road in 1857, and moved to Bromley Road, Catford, in 1925; following war damage they were amalgamated with Colfes c1952. The Hatcliffes Almshouses built at East Greenwich in 1857 have survived.

57. *Lewisham Park was laid out in the 1850s as a large private square for the residents of a series of large houses which were to be built around it; in fact, houses were in the early period built only along the west and north sides.

No 78 (57A) is the only survivor of the original development; it is a very handsome stuccoed house, probably c1860, with fine stonework and doorcase.

Proceeding clockwise round the street called Lewisham Park, note: **St Mauritius House**, nos 65/67, a great and quite amazing post-modernist pile built for the St Mauritius Housing Association 1995, with the centre tiered upwards to a circular tower and a zigzag shape along the front and sides.

Nos 31/52 are stately gabled red brick houses of 1905.

Nos 15/30 are fanciful stock brick pairs with strange doorcases, of c1890.

Along the High Street side there are now three high-rise blocks of 1964, as well as the **War Memorial (57B)**, a white obelisk of 1921.

The private square became a public park in 1965, and it is very pleasant, with some fine trees; the depression in the centre was once a gravel pit.

58. 359/361 Lewisham High Street, a large pair built c1835, though no 359 has been substantially altered and given a different facade since the war.

59. Mount Pleasant Road was laid out in the early 1870s; it has a fine series of imposing houses with strong gables, though nos 1/3 are Italianate.

60. The George, 1 Rushey Green. The L-shaped building at the front, though completely restored after the war, still preserves the appearance of the pub as it was c1800; however, the porch and the rear extension are postwar additions.

Adjacent, on the south side of **George Lane**, is an interesting group of houses of c1815. **Nos 2/6** are a terrace of small cottages; **nos 8/10** are a similar pair, though a modern shopfront spoils no 8. **Nos 18a, 20, 22** are a group set back behind long front gardens. **No 28** is a more substantial, originally detached house.

61. Thackerays Almshouses. A strange building, with gabled ends and a central romanesque archway. The inscription reads: 'Built and endowed 1840 for 6 aged females by John Thackeray of The Priory Lewisham who died 1851'. Thackeray's monument is in St Mary's Church; The Priory was a large house just north of the almshouses, the last part being demolished 1932.

62. Lewisham Hospital, to be renamed University Hospital Lewisham.

The Hospital began as the Lewisham Workhouse, a building of 1817 which now forms just the left-hand part, known as **Waterloo Block (62A)**, of the old entrance block to the south of the present main entrance. (The original 1817 keystone can be seen on the rear side of an archway in a corridor in the Waterloo Block marked

'Central Entrance'.) The right-hand part of the old entrance block is of 1885, the join clearly identifiable along the roofline; the projecting entrance porch, with a pediment inscribed 'Lewisham Union', is of 1887.

> The first Lewisham workhouse was set up in 1745. It was transferred to this site in 1817, and taken over by Lewisham Union in 1836. In the 1880s the workhouse was extended. Lewisham Infirmary was built to the north in 1894; though intended primarily for workhouse inmates, other patients were treated from the start. The workhouse and the infirmary were separated by a high wall. In 1915 they came together as Lewisham Military Hospital. In 1918 the wall was demolished, and the whole complex became Lewisham Hospital, though some workhouse use continued until 1929. Numerous new buildings have since been added, and a largescale development programme (including a new main entrance) is due for completion 1997.

To the north, the next large building fronting the High Street is the former **Doctors Quarters (62B)**, of 1895, now used as a paediatric unit and for offices; it is a more fanciful building, of stock brick with prominent red brick dressings, topped by a cupola. Going west inside the site, the present E Block of the Hospital survives from the original Infirmary of 1894, also of stock brick with prominent red brick dressings, though with modern glazed sections; note the water tower.

The stores building (which formerly incorporated a chapel) behind the old entrance is of 1885. The Medical Centre Clubroom, opposite the ambulance entrance to Accident & Emergency, was built for mentally ill patients in 1896.

These earlier buildings now form part of a large and complicated network, like a maze as one walks around the site. Amongst later buildings worthy of notice are the mental health unit, previously the nurses home, of 1927; the womens & childrens wing, of 1996; the boiler house, of 1986; and the mortuary, of 1993. In Accident & Emergency, a building of 1958, the foyer has a stained glass window by Faye Carey 1990 and a wooden sculpture Serendipity by Brian Willsher 1992.

The **former Lewisham Library (62C)**, built 1901 and closed 1994, has recently been absorbed into the Hospital as the Education Centre. It is an impressive red brick building, with a great entrance archway and tower above, and lots of terracotta decoration. Next door (outside the Hospital) is the Registrar's Office, on the site of Colfes Almshouses, demolished 1958 *(see 56)*.

From the Hospital southwards grass strips between the buildings and the main road mark the course of a stream which until 1855 ran the length of the High Street to join the Ravensbourne near Lewisham Bridge *(see Introduction, pages 69, 71)*.

63. **Church of St Mary the Virgin. A handsome Georgian ragstone church of 1777 by George Gibson, which retains to the west the late 15th century tower of the previous church. The effect is rather spoilt by the addition of an unattractive Victorian romanesque chancel by Sir Arthur Blomfield, which replaced a shallow apse in 1881.

> This was the original parish church of Lewisham. There has been a church on this site since at least 1100. The previous church was 15th century; its floor was on the level of the present crypt. It took from 1471 to 1502 to build the tower. In 1777 Gibson rebuilt the church, apart from the tower, to which he added an upper stage. The Victorian restoration of 1881 involved, in addition to the new chancel, the removal of the Georgian ceiling, apse, and west gallery.

The main entrance portico facing the High Street is particularly striking with its four powerful columns under a large pediment; note the unusual capitals. To the right, above a window, is a much eroded tablet to Abraham Colfe 1657 *(see 56)*.

To the tower, with its Gothic windows, Gibson added a Georgian upper stage with elegant classical ornamentation. The stonework around the west tower door and window were replaced in 1907, the doorway being re-erected in the garden of Ladywell House *(see 48)*.

The *interior is rather disappointing, resulting almost entirely from the Victorian restoration, though there are some interesting monuments, some from the previous church. *(The church is often open 1000-1100 Thursdays, otherwise contact the Vicarage at 48 Lewisham Park, or ring 0181-690 2682.)*

The archway into the tower is Gothic. The floor under the tower is much lower, showing the lower level of the earlier church. The elaborate font is of 1881. All the stained glass is of the early 1950s, by A. L. Wilkinson.

The chancel of 1881 is approached under a very tall round-headed chancel arch; it is very ornate, with a mosaic reredos, a series of mosaic figures, and numerous small romanesque windows. The altar is of Purbeck marble 1995. The sanctuary is raised and tiered, the first rounded step behind the altar indicating the position of the Georgian apse.

Numerous wall monuments and tablets line the aisles on the ground floor, and the galleries above - access to the north gallery is via the original Georgian staircase in the sacristy, to the south gallery from the porch. The following are noteworthy. In the north aisle, over the sacristy doorway, a tablet to Margaret Colfe 1643; to the west of the doorway, Mary Lushington 1797, a really fine flowing composition by John Flaxman, and Dean George Stanhope 1728 *(see New Cross 33)*; and to its east, a small brass to George Hatcliffe 1514. In the south aisle Thomas Wilkieson 1786, with an interesting inscription. In the north gallery, at the west end, Anne Petrie 1787, a framed deathbed group by Van Pook of Brussels. In the south gallery, at the west end, Margaret Petrie 1791, by Thomas Banks, another framed deathbed scene. Above the tower archway, and difficult to see as the west gallery is no longer there, an ornate and complex monument to John Thackeray 1851 *(see 61)* by E. H. Baily.

The *churchyard is highly attractive, split into two sections with a footpath running through, and mostly surrounded by a mainly 18th century wall, with many tombs and gravestones remaining. Just past the tower is the distinctive tomb to Ephraim How, a pioneer in British cutlery manufacture at a mill at Southend, Lewisham, in the early 18th century. The footpath continues to Ladywell Fields and a modern bridge over the River Ravensbourne.

64. Ladywell Fields was purchased for the public 1889, and is in three parts. A footpath throughout follows the course of (though not always providing close views of) the River Ravensbourne, which is more attractive here than elsewhere in Lewisham, as the river bed and the banks mostly retain a natural appearance. Wagtails and kingfishers can be seen here. The first field, nearest St Mary's Churchyard, is ancient and large. Then you come to a great bridge c1994 which snakes up and over the Mid Kent Line. The next field leads up to the old admin block of Ladywell Lodge *(see 39C)*. Then you pass under a bridge of the Catford Loop Line, beyond which is the third and largest field.

LEWISHAM

Suggested Walks

It is recommended that the suggested walks be followed in conjunction with the Gazetteer and the maps, and that the Gazetteer be consulted at each location for a detailed description. Most locations described in the Gazetteer are covered; some other locations have not been included, as they might add too much to the length of the walks.

Walk no 1 covers Section 'A', and Walk no 2 Section 'B'. The walks follow a more or less circular route, so can be joined at any location. Walk no 1 begins and ends at Lewisham Station, and Walk no 2 at Ladywell Station.

WALK no 1 (including Lewisham Town Centre and Loampit Hill). Distance approx 3 kilometres.

NB. It is worth trying to make an advance arrangement - see the Gazetteer - to view the interior of St Stephens Church.

On leaving **Lewisham Station (1)**, note work in progress on construction of the Docklands Light Railway station on part of the **Lewisham Bus Station (2)** site opposite. Turn left down the footpath alongside the North Kent Line, go under the railway arch and turn sharp left along **Silk Mills Path (3)**, noting **nos 1/6** and **Sharsted Villas**. Continue, bear right round the **Tesco Store (4)** to Lewisham Road, cross the road at the traffic lights and turn right.

Note **Eagle House** on the right, pass the **obelisk (5A)**, note **Heath Terrace (5)** on the right, and continue under the railway arch into **Lewisham High Street**, keeping to the left (east) side. Note **nos 15/31 (7)** and the **Church of St Stephen (8)**; try to see the interior. Continue past the empty sites of the Army & Navy store to **Yates's Wine Lodge (9)**, and note **nos 85/93 (10)** opposite. If you have time, proceed along **Lee High Road (11)** for some way and return.

Cross into the pedestrianised area to the **Clock Tower (15)** and **Lewisham Market (16)**; further south, note the entrance to The Lewisham Centre, to be visited later in the walk. Continue along Lewisham High Street to **St Saviours Church (17)**, look at the interior, and then to **Prudential Buildings (18)**. Turn left along **Limes Grove (19)** as far as no 38, return, and visit **Lewisham Library (20)**.

Note **Camden Villas (23)** opposite and the **Ridgeway** sculpture, cross the road, then proceed a short distance on the right side of **Molesworth Street (24)**; opposite are **Riverdale Mill** and **Riverdale House**. Turn right into **Lewisham Model Market (25)**, through to the High Street and turn left, noting **no 194** on the corner. Enter **The Lewisham Centre (26)** through the C&A store (if it is open), otherwise further along though the main entrance. Walk through the Centre, and at the northern end bear left and out into Molesworth Street; continue to Loampit Vale, noting **Lewisham Bridge (2A)**, then turn left under the railway arch of the Mid-Kent Line.

88

At Algernon Road, turn left for **Bibleway Tabernacle (27)** and return to Loampit Vale. You then pass **The Angel (28)** and ascend Loampit Hill to **Halesworth Road (29)**; note also **Shell Road** and **Loampit Gospel Hall (30)** at this point. Continue to Tyrwhitt Road, then cross the road to **The Old Station (31)**. Turn right down Loampit Hill, note **nos 64/70** and **no 62 (32)**, go into **Somerset Gardens (33)** and return, pass **Sunninghill Terrace (34)**. Turn left into **Elswick Road** and bear round past **no 28 (35)** back into Loampit Vale, turn left and continue until you are back at Lewisham Station.

WALK no 2 (including Ladywell, Lewisham Park, Lewisham Hospital and St Mary's Church). Distance approx 3 kilometres.

It is worth making an advance arrangement - see the gazetteer - to view the interior of St Marys Church.

On leaving **Ladywell Station (36)**, walk up to Ladywell Road, and note **Ladywell Bridge (37)** over the railway and river. Turn left, noting the buildings of **Ladywell Village (38)** between the **Foresters Arms** and **Ladywell Tavern**. To the left is Slagrove Place; if you have time, go through the gateway to see the remaining and the new buildings of **Ladywell Lodge (39)**, then return. Continue along Ladywell Road to the site of the Mineral Spring at **no 148 (40)** and the gates of **Ladywell Cemetery (41)**. Return along the north side of Ladywell Road, and make a short detour up Vicars Hill and **Algernon Road (42)**.

Beyond Ladywell Bridge, note the terraces along Ladywell Street and **Church Grove (38A)**. As you continue, note the sequence of buildings opposite - **St Mary's Centre (43)**, the **former Ladywell Baths (44), Lewisham Coroners Court (45), Lewisham Police Station (46)**, and the **former Lewisham Fire Station (47)**. On the corner as you turn left into Lewisham High Street is **Ladywell House (48)**.

Adjoining Ladywell House are **286/324 Lewisham High Street (49)**, and beyond are **nos 270/272 (50)**. Cross the road to **Jasmine Bingo Club (51)**, then turn right along the east side of the High Street, passing **Lewisham United Reformed Church (52)**, the premises of **H.E. Olby (53)**, **nos 315/317 (54)**, and then **St Mary's School (55)**.

At the corner with **Lewisham Park (57)**, note **Colfe and Hatcliffe Glebe (56)**, and turn left to **no 78 (57A)**. Cross into the park and walk to the other side, turn right for Lewisham High Street, then left. You pass **nos 359/361 (58)** and **Mount Pleasant Road (59)** before reaching **The George (60)**; walk along George Lane as far as **no 28**, then return.

Cross the road to **Thackerays Almshouses (61)**. Turn right for **Lewisham Hospital (62)**. Note the **Waterloo Block (62A)**, then continue along the High Street, passing the former **Doctors Quarters (62B)** and the **former Lewisham Library (62C)**, until you reach **St Mary's Church (63)**; try to see the interior. Follow the footpath through the **churchyard** and into **Ladywell Fields (64)**; the footpath quickly takes you back to Ladywell Station. (If you have time, walk through Ladywell Fields along the River Ravensbourne; this walk also leads to the Ladywell Lodge buildings.)

Notes on some Architects & Artists

(Gazetteer references - D = Deptford; NC = New Cross; B = Brockley; L = Lewisham)

Thomas Archer, c1668-1743 *(D 3)*. An architect in an uncompromising baroque style. His works were relatively few but were outstanding. They include St Pauls Deptford, St Johns Smith Square, Birmingham Cathedral, and Roehampton House.

Sir Arthur Blomfield, 1829-99 *(B 8, L 63)*. An architect of the Victorian Gothic revival. His works included the Royal College of Music and Selwyn College, Cambridge, as well as numerous churches. The firm of Sir Arthur Blomfield & Son continued to do important work after his death.

Sir Reginald Blomfield, 1856-1942 *(NC 28)*. Nephew of Sir Arthur Blomfield. From 1895 he became an advocate of Edwardian neo-classicism. He designed the Regent Street quadrant and the western part of Piccadilly Circus.

James Brooks, 1825-1901 *(L 27)*. An important architect of the Gothic Revival, who designed numerous tall and austere churches in London.

Sir Edwin Cooper, 1873-1942 *(D 25A)*. Architect of the Edwardian classical revival, who reacted against the more baroque forms. He designed the Port of London Authority building, and the Star & Garter home at Richmond.

Thomas Dinwiddy, 1845-c1926 *(NC 28A)*. An architect of South-East London. He designed the Laurie Grove Baths, New Cross; the Roan School for Girls, Greenwich; The Hollies, Sidcup; and Grove Park Hospital.

John Flaxman, 1755-1826 *(L 63)*. One of the leading classical sculptors of his time, and a prolific sculptor of monuments, which are in St Pauls Cathedral, Westminster Abbey, and many Central London and suburban churches.

Thomas Ford *(D 23)*. An architect who has since the war built many churches and carried out many restorations, often with rather startling interiors, in South London.

Sir Frederick Gibberd *(L 24)*. A noted modern architect, whose Pullman Court Streatham was a prewar example of the modernist style. The postwar works of Sir Frederick Gibberd & Partners have been more eclectic - they have included the earlier buildings of Heathrow Airport; early buildings in Harlow New Town; Coutts Bank; Liverpool Roman Catholic Cathedral; Regents Park Mosque.

Grinling Gibbons, 1648-1721 *(D 23)*. An outstanding woodcarver (and monumental sculptor), who lived and worked in Deptford in the early part of his life. His woodwork is in many buildings by Sir Christopher Wren. Much good woodwork of his time has been attributed to him.

George Gibson *(D 46, L 63)*. A Georgian architect of South East London, responsible for three major buildings in the area - St Mary's Church Lewisham; Woodlands Blackheath; and Stone House Deptford, where he himself lived. The capitals on columns in each building are unusual and similar.

ARCHITECTS & ARTISTS - 91

Philip Charles Hardwick, 1820-90 *(D 47)*. Son of the more famous Philip Hardwick. He designed St Johns Church Deptford and Great Western Hotel Paddington, and (together with his father) the demolished Great Hall of Euston Station.

Lanchester & Rickards *(NC 27)*. Henry Lanchester (1863-1953) and Edwin Rickards (1872-1920) formed this famous partnership specialising in the Edwardian Baroque. Originally called Lanchester, Stewart & Rickards, but James Stewart died in 1902. The partnership designed Cardiff City Hall & Law Courts; Westminster Central Hall; and Deptford Town Hall.

George Landmann, 1780-1854 *(D 1, 12B)*. The engineer who designed the viaduct and stations for the London & Greenwich Railway, the first passenger railway in London.

John Maine *(D 6, L 24)* was appointed as artist to Lewisham 2000, and was involved in the design of many projects carried out during the improvement scheme and afterwards.

Sir Charles Nicholson, 1867-1949 *(L 8)*. Architect of numerous churches in avariety of styles throughout the country.

Joseph Nollekens, 1737-1823 *(D 3)*. A distinguished classical sculptor, who was considered the leading portrait sculptor of his time. There are numerous works by him in Westminster Abbey.

Sir George Gilbert Scott, 1811-78 *(L 8)*. One of the most prolific architects in and propagandists for the Victorian Gothic style. His work, a major contribution to the London scene, included St Pancras Station, the Albert Memorial, and the Foreign Office (where Lord Palmerston insisted on a classical style). His numerous churches included St Mary Abbots at Kensington and St Giles at Camberwell, and he was a major restorer at Westminster Abbey.

Sir Giles Gilbert Scott, 1880-1960 *(L 13)*. Grandson of Sir George Gilbert Scott. Architect of Liverpool Anglican Cathedral, Battersea Power Station and Waterloo Bridge; and designer of the old red cast-iron telephone kiosks.

John Shaw, 1803-70 *(NC 28)*. A distinctive architect in the classical style, whose main works were colleges, including Goldsmiths College and Wellington College. He also designed the Jacobean frontages of Lamorbey House, Sidcup.

Leonard Stokes, 1858-1925 *(L 13A)*. A prolific architect in a variety of styles, but chiefly Arts & Crafts and neo-classical. He designed many telephone exchanges.

Sir Alfred Brumwell Thomas, 1868-1948 *(NC 31, 33)*. Leading architect of the High Edwardian Baroque, in which style he designed Belfast City Hall, and the Town Halls of Woolwich and Stockport. He was also the architect of Addey & Stanhope School, and Deptford Library.

Alexander Thomson, 1817-75 *(NC 3, 26)*. This great Glasgow architect was known as 'Greek' Thomson because his numerous houses, churches and commercial buildings usually adopted a Greek form. Egyptian motifs also recur in his work. None of his buildings have survived outside Scotland.

Bibliography

including books and publications consulted, and books recommended for further reading, especially for information on local history and architectural detail

London 2: South, by Bridget Cherry & Nikolaus Pevsner (Buildings of England series, Penguin Books, 1983)
Handbook to the Environs of London, by James Thorne (1876, republished 1970)
The Industrial Archaeology of South East London (Goldsmiths College Industrial Archaeology Group, 1982)
Retracing Canals to Croydon & Camberwell, by Brian Salter (Living History Publications 1986)
Turning the Tide, the History of Everyday Deptford, by Jess Steele (Deptford Forum Publishing 1993)
A Part of Deptford Past & Present, the Parish of Our Lady of the Assumption 1842-1992, by Father John Kenny (1992)
A Trip through Deptford (Deptford Discovery Team, 1996)
The Deptford Riverside. by Ken White, 1996
St Nicholas, the Ancient Parish Church of Deptford, by Myles Dove, 1996
Guide to the Ancient Parish Church of Deptford, St Nicholas, by Peter Gurnett, 1992
Guide to the Deptford Parish Church of St Paul, by Peter Gurnett, 1992
St Pauls Church Deptford, by Jennifer Mills (Lewisham Local History Society, 1983)
Churches in the Hundred of Blackheath, by L. A. J. Baker (Greenwich & Lewisham Antiquarian Society, 1961)
From the Marquis to the Obelisk, a Town Trail (Lewisham Local Studies Centre)
A Walk down the High Street (Lewisham Local Studies Centre)
From the Tiger to the Clock Tower, edited by Diana Rimel (Lee Community Education Centre, 1990)
Goldsmiths College, a Centenary Account, by A. E. Firth, 1991
Charing Cross to Orpington, by Vic Mitchell & Keith Smith (Middleton Press, 1991)
London Bridge to East Croydon, by Vic Mitchell & Keith Smith (Middleton Press)
London's First Railway, by R. H. G. Thomas (1972)
Looking back at Lewisham (Lewisham Local Studies Centre)
Lewisham History and Guide, by John Coulter (Alan Sutton Publishing, 1994)
A History of the Lewisham Silk Mills, by Sylvia Macartney and John West (Lewisham Local History Society 1979)
St Mary's Church Lewisham, a brief history, by Julian Watson, 1996
A History of St Stephens Lewisham, 1965
Old Ordnance Survey maps, published by Alan Godfrey - Deptford North 1914, New Cross 1914, Brockley 1868, Lewisham 1894
Many articles in Journals of the Greenwich Historical Society (formerly Greenwich & Lewisham Antiquarian Society), and of the Lewisham Local History Society

All the above publications, and of course many more books, maps and documents, can be consulted at **Lewisham Local Studies Centre**, Lewisham Library, Lewisham High Street, London SE13 (phone 0181-297 0682).

INDEX

(Gazetteer references - D = Deptford; NC = New Cross; B = Brockley; L = Lewisham)

Architects & Artists
Thomas Archer - D 3
E. H. Baily - L 63
Thomas Banks - L 63
Sir Arthur Blomfield - B 8; L 63
Sir Reginald Blomfield - NC 28
Broadway Malyan - D 17
James Brooks - L 27
Faye Carey - L 62
Christiani & Nielsen - D 27
Clayton & Bell - B 8; L 8
Annalisa Colombara - D 28
Sir Edwin Cooper - D 25A
Alfred Cross - L 32, 33
Thomas Dinwiddy - NC 28A
Gary Drostle - D 13B
Evelyn Dunbar - B 12A
James Edmeston - D 44
Mildred Eldridge - B 12A
John Flaxman - L 63
Thomas Ford - D 23
Sir Frederick Gibberd & Partners - L 24
Grinling Gibbons - D 23
George Gibson - D 46; L 63
Eric Gill - D 22
Greenaway & Newbery - B 22; L 13C
Frank Harding - L 8
Philip Charles Hardwick - D 47
Ron Haselden - L 20
John James - D 3
Jestico & Whiles - D 33A
Peter Kent - D 46
Sir Godfrey Kneller - D 23
Lanchester & Rickards - NC 27
Thomas Lucas - D 3, 4, 23
Charles Mahoney - B 12A
John Maine - D 6; L 24
Frederick Marrable - B 8
Violet Martin - B 12A
Edwin Nash - L 48
Sir Charles Nicholson - L 8
Joseph Nollekens - D 3
J. E. Nuttgens - L 8
Gerda Rubinstein - L 4
Sir George Gilbert Scott - L 8
Sir Giles Gilbert Scott - L 13A
Michael Searles - D 44B
William Snooke - NC 37, 38A
John Shaw - NC 28
South London Murals - D 2G
Stanley Spencer - B 12A
Charles Stanton - D 23
Henry Stock - NC 38B, 40
Leonard Stokes - L 13A
Sir Alfred Brumwell Thomas - NC 31, 33
Alexander Thomson - NC 3, 26
Henry Turner - D 3
Van Pook - L 63
Ward & Hughes - D 47
Sir Aston Webb - D 13
Amon Henry Wilds - NC 2D
A. L. Wilkinson - L 63
Brian Willsher - L 62
Alan Younger - D 3

Churches
All Saints - NC 5
Bibleway Tabernacle - L 27
Brockley Baptist - B 5A
Celestial Church - NC 18
College Park Baptist - L 13D
Deptford Methodist - D 20
Goldsmiths Chapel - NC 28
Kingdom Hall - NC 2A
Lewisham United Reformed - L 52
Loampit Gospel Hall - L 30
Olivet Deptford Baptist - NC 19
Our Lady of the Assumption - D 5
St Andrews - B 15
St Catherine - NC 40
St Hilda - B 22
St James - NC 28B
St Johns - D 47
St Lukes - D 37
St Marks Deptford - NC 18
St Marks Lewisham - L 13C
St Mary the Virgin - L 48, 63
St Mary Magdalens - B 17
St Nicholas - D 23
St Pauls - D 3
St Peters - B 8
St Saviours - L 17
St Stephen - L 8
Transfiguration - L 27
Welsh Presbyterian - D 48; L 30
Zion Baptist - NC 35

Housing developments
Burrells Wharf - D 33A
Colfe & Hatcliffe Glebe - L 56
College Park Estate - L 13
Crossfield Estate - D 12
Deptford Wharf - D 31
Gilmore Estate - L 13
Hatcham Manor Estate - NC 37
Mereton Mansions - D 9

94 - INDEX

Milton Court Estate - NC 22
Pepys Estate - D 30
St Mauritius House - L 57
St Nicholas House - D 24
Slagrove Place Estate - L 39
Somerville Estate - NC 8
Sylva Cottages - D 9A
Thackerays Almshouses - L 61
Vanguard Estate - D 42

Industrial archaeology
Armoury Mill - L 3
Borthwick Wharf - D 25A
Boundary stones, markers - D 32; NC 28, 38
Breweries - D 10; L 4
Bridge House Estate marks - B 12E; L 40
Burrells Wharf - D 33A
Clark Bunnett & Co - NC 36
Clock Tower - L 15
Convoys Wharf - D 27
Co-op Movement - L 9
Creekside - D 13, 15A, 17
Croydon Canal - D 34; NC 1; B 2, 13, 19
Deptford Bridge - D 10
Deptford Creek Bridge - D 14
Deptford Power Station - D 17
Deptford Pumping Station - D 40, 41
Docklands Light Railway - D 10, 40, 41; L 2
East India Company - D 17
Gas lamps - NC 36
General Steam Navigation Company - D 17
Gin Distillery - D 10A
Grand Surrey Canal - D 34; NC 11
Haberdashers Company - NC 2A/B, 37, 38, 40
Hatcham Iron Works - NC 7
Ladywell springs - L 37, 40
Letter boxes - D 38; L 36
Lewisham Silk Mills - L 3
Markets - D 2; L 16, 25
Mazawattee Tea Co - NC 11A
Mechanics Path - D 1B
New Cross Building Society - NC 34
New Cross Bus Depot - NC 2A
Old railway stations - B 14; L 31
Paynes Wharf - D 25
John Penn & Sons - D 25
Property marks - D 30A; NC 37, 38; B 12E, 18; L 40
Railway bridges - NC 10, 11, 13; B 13, 19
Railway ramp - D 1A
Railway Stations - D 1, 38; NC 1, 25; B 13, 20; L 1, 36
Railway viaducts - D 1, 12B; NC 16
Railway works & sidings - NC 1, 10
River access points - D 15A, 26, 30
Riverdale Mill - L 24A
Riverside walks - D 26, 30, 31, 33
Road bridges - D 10, 14, 34; B 2, 19; L 2, 37
Royal Naval Dockyard - D 27

Royal Victoria Victualling Yard - D 30
SELCHP - NC 14
Stones Works - NC 17
Stowage - D 17
Telephone kiosks - L 13A
Toilet ventilating pipes - NC 3, 26
Trade sign - NC 36
Trinity House - D 17
Water Towers - L 39B, 62
Workhouses - L 39, 62

Leisure
The Albany - D 2H
Former swimming baths - D 2C; NC 28A; L 44
Jasmine Bingo Club - L 51
Millwall Football Club - NC 10, 12, 13
Moonshot Community Centre - NC 23A
Old cinemas - D 2B; NC 2C, 26; B 20A
Rivoli Ballroom - B 20A
Theatres in pubs - D 11; B 21
Wavelengths - D 2G

Parks & open spaces
Bridge House Meadows - NC 13
Brockley Cemetery - B 18; L 41
Brookmill Park - D 41
Deptford Park - D 36
Folkestone Gardens - NC 15
Fordham Park - NC 23
Hilly Fields - B 12
Ladywell Cemetery - B 18; L 41
Ladywell Fields - L 64
Lewisham Park - L 57
Margaret McMillan Park - D 6
Memorial Gardens - D 44A
Sayes Court Park - D 28
Sue Godfrey Nature Park - D 12C
Telegraph Hill Park - NC 41

People
John Addey - D 23; NC 33
Robert Aske - NC 38
Sir Joseph Bazalgette - D 13A
Rose Bruford - D 18
Isambard Kingdom Brunel - D 33A
Dr Charles Burney - D 3
Abraham Colfe - L 6, 56, 63
Father David Diamond - D 3
Ralph Dodd - D 34
Sir Francis Drake - D 30
Leland Lewis Duncan - L 22
George England - NC 7
John Evelyn - D 23, 28
William Fairbairn - D 33A
Sebastian de Ferranti - D 17
James Elroy Flecker - L 13B
Hardcastle family - NC 2C, 5
William Hatcliffe - L 56
Ephraim How - L 63

Rudolph Laban - NC 28B
George Landmann - D 1, 12B
Jonathan Lucas - D 48
Margaret McMillan - D 19, 22; B 18
Rachel McMillan - D 19, 22; B 18
Christopher Marlowe - D 23
Edith Nesbit - L 35
John Penn - D 25
Peter the Great - D 2A, 17, 28
Josiah Stone - NC 17
Dean George Stanhope - NC 33; L 48, 63
Thankfull Sturdee - D 39B
John Tallis - NC 2
John Thackeray - L 61, 63
Edgar Wallace - B 10
Sir Barnes Wallis - NC 2
John Wesley - L 17
Henry Williamson - B 12B

Public buildings (present & former)
Crofton Park Library - B 20
Deptford Fire Station - D 37
Deptford Library - NC 31
Deptford Police Station - NC 20
Deptford Town Hall - NC 27
Lewisham Coroners Court - L 45
Lewisham Fire Station - L 47
Lewisham Hospital - L 62
Lewisham Library - L 20, 62
Lewisham Police Station - L 46
New Cross Fire Station - NC 8
New Cross Hospital - NC 6
New Cross Library - NC 2C
Old Town Library - D 2C
Telephone Exchange - L 13A

Pubs
Angel - L 28
Ballylane Inn (Pilot) - D 2A
Birds Nest (Oxford Arms) - D 11
Breakspeare Arms - B 1
Brockley Jack - B 21
Castle - L 49
Centurion - D 8
Cranbrook - D 39
Crown & Anchor - NC 2C
Crown & Sceptre - D 42
Dew Drop Inn - NC 23B
Dover Castle - D 8
Duke - D 16
Duke of Edinburgh - B 3
Five Bells - NC 2C
Flower of Kent - NC 29
Fox & Firkin (Black Bull) - L 49
Freemasons Arms - L 38
George - L 60
Goldsmiths Tavern - NC 26
Harp of Erin - D 21
Hatcham Arms - NC 2C
Hobgoblin (Rose of Lee) - L 11

Hoy Inn - D 15
Ladywell Tavern - L 38
Lord Wolseley - B 5
Maimie O'Learys (White Swan) - D 2B
Marquis of Granby - NC 26
Mechanics Arms - D 1
New Cross Inn - NC 26
Noahs Ark - D 2E
Noodle King (Fountain) - D 8
Paradise Bar (Royal Albert) - NC 36
Pitchers (Plough) - L 2
Princess of Wales - D 28
Rose Inn - NC 2B
Rosemary Branch - NC 29
Sultan - L 11
Talbot - B 11
Walpole - NC 36B
White Hart - NC 3
White Horse - L 11
Wickham Arms - B 5
Yates's Wine Lodge - L 9

Schools, colleges etc
Addey & Stanhope School - NC 33
Childeric School - NC 24
Deptford Park School - D 35
Edmund Waller School - NC 39
Goldsmiths College - NC 27-29, B 1
Haberdashers Askes Hatcham College - NC 38A/B
Laban Centre - NC 28B
Lewisham Academy of Music - D 6
Lewisham College - D 8, 45
Lucas Vale School - D 43A
Mornington Centre - NC 36A
Prendergast School - B 12
Rachel McMillan Building - D 19
Rachel McMillan Nursery School - D 22
Rose Bruford College - D 18
St Mary's School - L 55

Streets
Adelaide Avenue - B 12, 16
Admiral Street - D 39
Albury Street - D 4
Albyn Road - D 39
Algernon Road - L 27, 42
Algiers Road - L 42
Amersham Grove - NC 21
Amersham Road - NC 29
Amersham Vale - NC 20, 25
Arklow Road - NC 17, 19
Avon Road - B 10
Bolden Street - D 39B
Borthwick Street - D 25, 26
Breakspears Road - B 9
Brighton Grove - NC 1A
Brockley Cross - B 14
Brockley Road - B 13, 15, 18, 20-22
Brookmill Road - D 9, 10, 40, 41

96 - INDEX

Church Grove - L 38A
Clarendon Rise - L 13C/D
Cliff Terrace - D 39
Clyde Street - D 2C
Coldblow Lane - NC 10
Copperas Street - D 13
Coulgate Street - B 1
Cranbrook Road - D 39
Creek Road - D 14-16, 18-21
Creekside - D 13
Crescent Way - B 10
Cressingham Road - L 8
Darling Road - B 10
Deptford Broadway - D 8
Deptford Church Street - D 8, 11, 12A
Deptford Green - D 23, 24
Deptford High Street - D 1-3, 5
Douglas Way - D 2G/H
Drake Road - B 10
Eastdown Park - L 12
Eastern Road - B 12B
Edward Street - NC 16, 18
Elswick Road - L 35
Embleton Road - L 42
Erlanger Road - NC 37, 41
Ermine Road - L 42
Evelyn Street - D 2E, 34B, 37
Florence Road - NC 30
Friendly Street - D 42
George Lane - L 60
Giffin Street - D 2G
Gilmore Road - L 13A/B
Glensdale Road - B 7
Granville Grove - L 8
Grove Street - D 27A, 29, 30
Halesworth Road - L 29
Hatcham Park Road - NC 4
Hilly Fields Crescent - B 12D
Jerningham Road - NC 37, 38
Kender Street - NC 7
Kitto Road - NC 41
Ladywell Road - L 37, 38, 40, 41, 43-48
Lamerton Street - D 2C
Laurie Grove - NC 28A
Lee High Road - L 11
Lewisham High Street - L 7-10, 15-18, 20, 23, 25, 26, 49-56, 58, 61-63
Lewisham Park - L 57
Lewisham Road - L 4, 5
Lewisham Way - D 44-48; NC 29, 31
Limes Grove - L 18, 19
Lingards Road - L 22
Loampit Hill - L 28, 31, 32, 34
Lucas Street - D 43
Ludwick Mews - NC 22A
Malpas Road - B 3
Manor Avenue - B 6
Mercia Grove - L 14
Molesworth Street - L 24
Mount Pleasant Road - L 59

Nettleton Road - NC 2A
New Cross Road - NC 1-3, 5, 25-27, 33-36
Parkfield Road - NC 29
Pepys Road - NC 37, 38, 40, 41
Prince Street - D 27, 28
Queens Road - NC 8, 9
Rokeby Road - B 4
St Donatts Road - B 1
St Johns Vale - D 39
St Margarets Road - B 16
St Stephens Grove - L 8
Shardeloes Road - B 2
Shell Road - L 29
Silk Mills Path - L 3
Slagrove Place - L 39A
Slaithwaite Road - L 21
Somerset Gardens - L 33
Stowage - D 17
Strickland Street - D 39
Sunninghill Road - L 34
Surrey Canal Road - NC 11
Tanners Hill - D 7; NC 32
Tressillian Crescent - B 10
Tressillian Road - B 10
Tyrwhitt Road - B 11
Upper Brockley Road - B 5
Vesta Road - NC 38; B 2
Vicars Hill - B 12C; L 42
Walerand Road - L 6
Waller Road - NC 37, 39
Watson Street - D 6
Wickham Road - B 7, 8
Woodpecker Road - NC 22